A Primer on the

ECONOMICS OF CONSUMPTION

A Primer on

The Primer series is under the editorial supervision of

PETER L. BERNSTEIN

the ECONOMICS
of CONSUMPTION

Elizabeth W. Gilboy

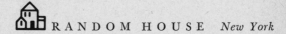 RANDOM HOUSE *New York*

In Memory of my
Father *and* Mother

The unprecedented concentration of discretional purchasing power in the hands of the consumer has put the household sector in a position of greater importance within the framework of the economy than it ever held.

Elizabeth Gilboy interprets the principal elements of theoretical and factual analysis in the field of the economics of consumption and presents them in a form accessible not only to a student of economics but to an interested general public as well.

WASSILY LEONTIEF

Acknowledgments

I should first like to thank Peter Bernstein, the editor, for his humorous and untiring efforts to show me how this primer should be written. It was quite an experience to learn how to present technical material in nontechnical terms. Professor Hendrik Houthakker was kind enough to read the manuscript and tell me that he liked it. I am indebted to him for many critical comments and suggestions. I also owe a debt to the students who have taken my course in the past few years and who have assisted me by their reactions in class in culling over the material to be presented. And, finally, I am in great debt to Mrs. Irene Raught, who typed the manuscript in its various stages and made editorial and other suggestions that were of ineffable value to me in the process.

Contents

A Primer on the

ECONOMICS OF CONSUMPTION

Introduction

The demands and expenditures of consumers are most important in a highly industrial economy such as that of the United States. Indeed, for the past few years, two-thirds of our total output of goods and services has been taken by consumers.

What determines consumption is not simple to explain in an economy such as ours or that of other developed countries. We are all consumers, of course, but do we know why we select both the kinds and qualities of things we purchase? Are we aware of the way consumption has grown—and changed—since the American economy was in its infancy? Are we familiar with what has happened to consumption in other countries?

A great deal of information exists on various aspects of consumption. I have selected certain significant elements in the consumer area, which, I hope, will shed light on these questions and also provide a basis for understanding the role of consumption in the field of economics.

Consumption is an area in which a large amount of disagreement exists. Is it a stimulus in itself to economic growth, or is it simply the result of changes in production techniques? What are the principal variables that motivate consumers to buy various products? How can we measure them? Even in the case of income and price, which are strictly economic variables, considerable differences of opinion occur as to just how these variables should be defined or how they influence consumers' decisions.

In the first three chapters, questions of this sort are considered. Chapter 1 attempts to define consumption and to discuss the various criteria that can be used in its measurement. Consumption theory is taken up in Chapter 2, starting with the theories of the classical and neoclassical economists of the nineteenth century. These economists emphasized the effects of income and price on the spending decisions of individuals and families. However, more modern economists have rather special definitions of "income," and these are also discussed in some detail. Attention is given to the equally modern "decision-making" school, which introduces a great number of noneconomic variables, such as demographic, sociological, or psychological forces, in addition to income and price. Chapter 3 is a factual analysis of what has actually happened to consumer incomes and expenditures in the United States since 1935–1936. Various consumer purchases studies (United States

Bureau of Labor Statistics) are used to indicate the significant changes in incomes and expenditures that have occurred since the Great Depression.

Chapter 4 deals with the concept of "leisure," both as a consumer perquisite and as a part of individual and national income. As hours at work are cut down, as they have been over the past hundred years, this concept becomes increasingly important.

In Chapter 5, changes in the size distribution of income from 1929 to the present are discussed, with some consideration of the implications of these changes. Measures of income inequality are also taken up, as well as the rapid growth of millionaires since World War II.

Chapter 6 is in three parts. The first of these deals with technological changes in consumption in the United States. Dorothy Brady's analysis of how an innovation in the consumer goods field is introduced into the market is discussed, as well as what has actually happened to the American diet over the last eighty years—a remarkable story of technological change. Second, Professor Hendrik Houthakker's analysis of Engel's laws (outlined in Chapter 1) as they apply to many countries in various stages of economic development are reviewed. And, finally, an analysis of what is happening to the consumer goods area in the Russian economy, based on recent experiments, is described. This last chapter can be looked upon as a study of the relation of changes in consumption to economic development in a number of countries.

It is hoped that this book will give the intelligent lay-man and student some idea as to what the problems are in the area of the economics of consumption. Consumption is important in our economy today, as it is in Western Europe and Japan. It is becoming important in the Soviet Union and other Eastern European countries. And, as economic growth takes place, consumption will increase and its problems will become significant for the underdeveloped countries all over the world.

Of course, consumption is important to any country, no matter what stage of growth it may have attained. But at a low level of industrial development, consumption can only provide some kind of subsistence standard of living for the majority of the population. *There is very little choice as to what consumers can buy at this stage.* With economic growth and the development of industrial sectors, however, the consumer area begins to expand. Incomes will rise, and new products will appear in consumer markets. The standard of living will go up, and a wide variety of consumer goods will eventually compete with one another for a place in the consumer budget.

In a highly developed economy, such as that of the United States, France, or West Germany, consumption is particularly significant for two reasons. The consumer has an almost infinite variety of consumer goods from which to choose and, at the same time, personal consumer expenditures have become relatively the largest part of the total output of final goods and services produced by the economy. This means that what the consumer chooses to buy has considerable effect not only upon national income, but also upon the outputs of individual industries.

CHAPTER 1

Consumption and the Economy as a Whole

The relationship between consumption and the rest of the economy is highly complex. Perhaps that is why the classical economists tended to emphasize production and neglect the consumer area. Furthermore, the fact that consumption does not usually become dynamically important for the economy as a whole until a certain stage of economic growth is reached is another reason for its neglect by classical economists. In the early days of industrialization, consumers' wants are not particularly emphasized: The major effort is placed on developing the techniques of production. As industrialization proceeds, however, the incomes of workers rise, and eventually they look around to see what additional consumer goods they can buy. New consumer goods may come from foreign trade—as they did in eighteenth-century England—or an attempt may be made to develop consumer industries at home. An outstanding modern example of such a development of the consumer goods industries is now taking place in the Soviet Union.

Whatever the reason, with economic growth, the shifting patterns of demand among consumers tend to become more important in the economy, and industrialists watch consumer buying habits with close attention. They are also concerned, of course, with changing these buying habits through the introduction of new and additional consumer goods. The process by which such new goods are introduced into the consumer market will be taken up in a later chapter.

In many ways the analysis of production is much easier than that of consumption. The productive process is determined largely by technical variables that are concrete and can be measured. If steel is to be made by the open-hearth method, for example, the necessary ingredients and their amounts are known, the timing of the various stages of production is given, and eventually steel plate or some other finished steel product rolls off the production line.

Although we know that consumers must buy some kind of food and clothing and housing, we cannot be sure just what particular goods within these categories they will purchase. They also are likely nowadays to have a car and various household durable goods. In making a choice in the market place, the individual or family will pay some attention to the price of the good and their own income. These are strictly economic variables and can be measured. However, there are a host of other variables that will also influence their choice: where they live, how large a family they have, the occupation of the chief wage earner, their expectations as to the future, what their neighbors or business associates have, whether they happen to like the particular products, and so on. Many of the variables are sociological, demographic, or psychological and are not strictly measurable in a technical sense.

The definition of consumption, or the household sector of the economy, is therefore more difficult than that of production. We know that most families will buy a car, but whether it will be a Volkswagen, a Chevrolet, or a Chrysler, we cannot be sure. Ramblers were rising in popularity several years ago; now they are declining. More people are moving to outer metropolitan areas. What effect will this have on the purchase of homes and the use of transportation systems? Questions of this kind are always coming up in the analysis of consumption, particularly in the case of a highly developed and industrialized economy such as that of the United States.

Strictly speaking, the household sector of an economy is usually defined as embracing the activities of consumers who buy the final goods and services produced by the economic system. Such final goods and services are represented by personal consumption expenditures in the national accounts of the economy, which are also equivalent to gross national product. The national accounts also include gross private domestic investment, government purchases of goods and services, and net exports of goods and services. Personal consumption expenditures in the United States, which are our chief concern, are by far the largest part of gross national product, having consistently amounted to two-thirds of the total in recent years.

If the elements of government expenditures that benefit the general public, such as those on education, public roads, national parks, and various recreational expenditures, were added to personal consumption expenditures, the percentage of gross national product that contributes to the level of living of consumers would be considerably greater. Strictly speaking, however, the household sector is ordinarily limited to the activities of consumers who buy, by their own choice, the final products of industry.

In fact, the spending activities of consumers cannot always be separated from their role as producers, since a great many consumers are producers as well. Although the functions of consuming and producing are now largely separated—most consumers do not produce directly for their own needs, as in a simple agricultural economy—the separation of the influences of consuming and producing on the decision to buy particular goods is not easy to make. A car, for example, may be needed as transportation to work as well as for recreation and vacation trips. This merging—or confusion —of the producing and consuming functions in spending is worth noting, since difficulties in the empirical analysis of consumer expenditures may very well result from it.

The consumption or household sector may be considered in terms of the individual consumer, the individual household, or the entire sector itself. Traditionally, the individual consumer is the unit for the neoclassical theory of economic welfare, which is summarized in the next chapter. Some recent attempts have been made to adapt neoclassical theory to a family or household unit, but they have not been entirely successful, as we shall see.

The individual consumer unit may be approached statistically when the consumer expenditure series of the Department of Commerce, for example, is used over the years (the figures go back to 1929). In this case, the total expenditure of each item is divided by the size of the population, and the expenditure series is transformed into per capita terms. However, many empirical studies of consumer behavior are in terms of the family or household unit. Such studies are usually of the cross-section variety, in which, at any one specific time, a statistical sample of individual families or households is interviewed and their family income and detailed expenditures on various consumer goods recorded. From this information, the families can be ranked according to income with their individual expenditures at these income levels given. (A number of these studies made by the Bureau of Labor Statistics [consumer purchases studies] will be examined in later chapters.)

Such cross-section studies may differ considerably in their definition of the household unit. For example, the Bureau of Labor Statistics uses a family unit in which all persons living together are included. At the University of Michigan, which has its own series of cross-section data, a spending unit is used in which all those who contribute to the income of the family are counted as members of the household. Consumer expenditures for the whole economy may be taken as the unit and related to aggregate or total income in the economy. John Maynard Keynes used this aggregate concept.

Many widely different variables determine consumer spending, although, historically, in the theoretical literature, price and income are preeminent. In addition, wealth and demographic and sociological variables, such as region, age, family size, race, city size, kind of job, are of considerable importance. Psychological variables may also be added, although some economists tend to question both their measurement and their value in the analysis of consumer spending.

The detailed analysis of consumption has been of relatively modern concern. Alfred Marshall, for example, attempted to redress the balance of supply and demand by dealing explicitly with consumption as well as with production. But he still believed fundamentally that the supply side, production, was the dominant economic force. He did admit that the basic needs and wants of a population must be satisfied, yet he thought essentially that changes in production stimulated new wants, and not that new wants changed production techniques. In his economic philosophy, production led and consumption followed.

John Maynard Keynes showed traces of this influence, despite his emphasis on consumption and its relationship to total income. His own theory is couched primarily in aggregative terms, that is, terms dealing with total investment as well as total consumption. Knowledge of the effects on the economy of these aggregates is highly necessary, but it is equally important to break income and consumption down into their component parts. In other words, the structure of consumption and other aggregates has great significance. If consumer expenditures increase, for example, the economic effects may be quite different, depending on the particular goods for which the consumer spends his income. Is he going to buy a new automobile or take a trip to Europe? This makes a considerable difference to the economy. If many consumers buy new automobiles, production in the auto industries will expand, thereby affecting all the industries down the line—even possibly stimulating new investment, if these industries are operating at capacity. Similarly, if the consumer prefers a trip to Europe, the international trade balance may be affected. Indeed, if enough people do this the gold outflow might increase, as a result of consumer spending in other countries. The United States government, in fact, recently felt sufficiently concerned about such spending abroad to reduce the tax-free allowance for goods purchased abroad.

We can make good estimates of the items consumers are most likely to buy if their incomes increase. Equally, if their incomes decrease, we can identify the expenditures that will tend to continue and those that will probably decrease. By taking some abstract indicator of the relation between income and expenditures, such as the percentage of income spent on each category, we can see the relation of changes in consumer purchases to changes in their incomes. Such percentages are usually derived from cross-section data in which family expenditures are classified according to income levels. From these data, we can compute income-expenditure curves that will indicate the percentage of income spent on each item at each income level.

Income-expenditure curves of this sort are called Engel curves, from the Prussian statistician Ernst Engel, who was the first to make them (in the late nineteenth century). Using Belgian cross-section data for the incomes and expenditures of certain clerical groups, he took broad categories, such as food, clothing, housing, and luxuries, and computed the percentage of income spent at each income level. These relationships have come to be known as Engel's laws, although Engel himself is responsible only for the one on food.

ENGEL'S LAWS:

1. Percentage spent on food decreases as income rises.
2. Percentage spent on housing stays about the same.

3. Percentage spent on clothing stays the same (or increases).
4. Percentage spent on luxuries increases.

Another measure of the income-expenditure relationship can be made by computing income-expenditure elasticities from the data. In this case, the *percentage* change in expenditure is divided by the *percentage* change in income, thereby determining income-expenditure elasticity units for each budgetary item. On the basis of such income-expenditure elasticities, Engel's laws would look like this:

Food	< 1	inelastic
Housing	1	unit elasticity
Clothing	1 or $>$	possibly elastic
Luxuries	> 1	elastic

These wide groups may be broken down into individual items, if sufficient data are available and the income percentages and elasticities calculated. This is now frequently done.

In these broad categories, the "laws" still stand. Within the main groups, however, the elasticities of individual items vary greatly. In the United States, for instance, expenditure on meat and fruits tends to be income elastic, although for food as a whole the expenditure is income inelastic.

The principal data available for the analysis of consumption consist of the Department of Commerce time

series and the Bureau of Labor Statistics consumer purchases studies, which started, in an embryonic way, in
1889. In using these data over a long time period, various problems arise. How can consumer expenditures
for, say, 1900, be compared with those for 1950 or 1960
in order to measure whether economic well-being has
increased? From a qualitative point of view, very different expenditure patterns are involved: There are
new commodities, a whole new complex of durable
goods such as cars, televisions, washing machines, or
dishwashers, and new materials and new processing.
Practically every kind of food is now sold in plastic
bags. It could be said that a certain percentage of income has been spent on basic consumer categories over
time but that the identification of structural changes
in consumption (and, in fact, the mixture of services,
such as precooking, into some consumer goods) requires
detailed cross-section studies. Such changes should be
related to technological changes in industry where possible. A somewhat similar problem exists when consumer expenditures are compared among countries in
different stages of economic development whose stand-
ards of living vary greatly.

We have stated previously that personal consumer
expenditures, which include all final sales to the household sector of the economy, are the largest item in our
national accounts, which cover as well the amounts
spent by government, business firms, and foreigners.
Now, national accounts are integrated with industrial
accounts in an input-output table for 1958, which has

been prepared by the United States Department of Commerce, Office of Business Economics. (Tables for 1961 and 1963 are also being prepared.) These industrial accounts list the purchases and sales that the industrial sectors have made to each other. Initiated by Professor Wassily Leontief at Harvard University, input-output tables are rapidly increasing in use throughout the world.[1] The essence of an input-output table lies in the fact of its disaggregation. The main operating part of the system is contained in that part of the input-output table that includes the individual industrial sectors of the economy. The sales of each such sector to itself, to all other industrial sectors of the economy, and to final demand, which is the equivalent of gross national product, are given. These are the rows. The columns indicate each industry's purchases, from itself and all other industries and from national income, which, again, equal gross national product. In its present state, an input-output table does not take into account the monetary aspect of the economy, although the figures are in monetary terms. Purely monetary flows are not dealt with as such.

In essence, the input-output system is one which is expressed in *real,* or physical, terms, although also expressed in dollars, or francs, or yen. Money serves only as a common denominator, to facilitate comparisons and computations. Each input or output is conceived

[1] See W. H. Miernyk's book for an elementary statement of the input-output system: *The Elements of Input-Output Analysis* (New York: Random House, 1965).

as the amount of a particular good or service that could be bought or sold for a unit of currency. In fact, physical quantities could be used and, indeed, have been by the Russians and others. This method, however, has a disadvantage: Although the rows can be added up, the columns cannot, which makes it impossible to solve the input-output system in mathematical terms.

The main concern of the input-output system is with the intermediate, or producing, sectors of the economy, which are left out of national accounts as double counting. However, a great deal of useful information on consumption and industry is revealed by the sales and purchases of each individual industry to and from each other, as well as to personal consumer expenditures and to final demand as a whole.

Consumption, or households, the largest part of final demand, is not usually included within the producing sectors of the economy. For certain problems, however, attempts have been made to include it.[2] If households *is* considered as an industry, its inputs are consumer expenditures and its outputs income received (largely wage income for the bulk of the population). Paul Samuelson once considered this possibility but dismissed it on the grounds that people ought not to be considered as machines that merely feed, clothe, and house themselves in order to produce labor services. One might well ask—why not?

[2] This has been done in certain regional input-output studies for the United States by the Harvard Economic Research Project.

In excluding households from the technical parts of the system, the repercussive effects of personal income induced by the final demand for consumer goods are lost. However, there are difficulties in including households as such an industry, not the least of which is the fact that many of the variables determining personal consumption are noneconomic, as we shall see.

A comparison of the input-output tables for 1947 and 1958 with respect to those industries that contributed very little to household consumption and those that contributed a great deal is of considerable interest.

Those industries contributing the least to final demand, it should be noted, are principally concerned with raw materials. This list has changed during the eleven-year period, in part due to some differences in classification; in part because of the greater uses of certain materials such as petroleum, leather, metal containers, and plastics by 1958.

A greater consistency exists among those industries that contribute the most to final demand. In both years, the trade, food, and rental industries head the list. Finance moved up above apparel in 1958, as did medical and educational services. Motor vehicles and electricity and gas and water appear in 1958 and not in 1947, indicating the large and increasing sale of automobiles and the extension of housing services.

Typically, the industries that give little or nothing to final demand are the basic producing industries. Those that give a large amount are the service industries, apparel, automobile, real estate, finance, and so on. It seems clear that the service industries have increased markedly over the period, as have motor vehicles.

With some notion, now, as to what the household sector of the economy is and how it may be defined and measured, we can go on and take up various aspects of consumption in greater detail. We should keep in mind, however, that our concept of consumption is by no means precise: The many economists who are concerned with the analysis of consumer purchasing habits characterize its definition and fundamental units quite differently.

After a summary discussion of the main categories of the theoretical developments and their implications, we will examine the concept of leisure as a consumer good, the use of the Bureau of Labor Statistics' consumer surveys, the effects of the changing shape of the size distribution of income (the population grouped according to income class), and the relationship between consumption and economic growth, especially in the United States and the Soviet Union.

CHAPTER 2

Consumption Theory

The theory of consumption has developed over the past sixty years and may be divided into three main parts: those that adhere to some form of the consumption function, or the relation between personal income and consumer expenditures; the theory of individual consumer preference, which differentiates the effects of income and price on consumers' spending decisions; and the more modern household decision-making school, which introduces a number of noneconomic variables, in addition to income and price, in an attempt to explain how households decide what and how much to buy.

The Consumption Function Approach

Consumption functions express the relationship between expenditures on consumer goods (either in the aggregate or for individual items) and income, with prices held constant. We find three different definitions of income for this purpose:[1] absolute income, relative income, and permanent income. Absolute income refers to the income which consumers receive at any one time and may be taken from published statistical data. Those who believe in relative income insist that consumers do not spend their money on the basis of current income, but on the basis of its relationship to their previous peak income or to the income of the community in which they live. Permanent income is defined as the income which an individual or family expects to have over their lifetime. Both absolute and relative income deal with current income, as derived from time series or cross-section data. Permanent income is a more complicated concept and difficult to measure from available statistics.

John Maynard Keynes first introduced the consumption function in his famous book *The General Theory of Employment, Interest, and Money* (1936). He was not so much interested in the income-spending relationship itself as in the postulates he derived from it. He began by assuming that consumers will both spend and save out of current income, never spending all their earnings on consumer goods. This is due to his "psychological law," which holds that people will tend to consume less than 100 percent of any increase in income and, consequently, that they will always tend to

---

[1] We have already seen, in Chapter 1, that the definition of consumption is a tricky matter, with many fuzzy edges.

save at least part of it. (In technical terms, we say that the marginal propensity to consume is less than one.) The law stipulates that the *amount* of saving will increase with each rise in income—and Keynes added the further suggestion that the *proportion* of income saved would also increase. Although this psychological law may not be true for every individual or family in the economy, it is probably correct for the majority of the population.

In attempting to test this hypothesis, contradictory results arose from the use of time series and cross-section data. Simon Kuznets' study of data going all the way back to 1870 showed that the percentage of aggregate income saved had in fact remained constant in the United States. On the other hand, studies of individual families with varying incomes at the same moment in time have indicated that the percentage of income saved is greater at higher income levels than at lower levels. While the cross-section data thus support Keynes, the time series data—covering the enormous rise in income since 1870—cast doubt upon his law.

James Duesenberry suggests that this inconsistency exists because the savings rate does not depend on absolute, but rather on *relative,* income. He pictures the consumer as constantly subjected to contact with the new and higher-quality goods that are bought by the groups around him. Each such contact demonstrates the superiority of these goods to those he has been buying, and, with a sufficient number of such contacts, the consumer will cut into his savings and will buy these new goods, even if income and prices do not change. In the long run, therefore, in periods of steadily rising income, the aggregate savings ratio tends to be independent of absolute income. In the short run, however, the savings ratio is tied, not to absolute income, but to the relationship of current income to previous peak income. If, for example, current income should go down, the consumer will, for a while at least, still buy the goods he bought at his previous income (or consumption) peak and will dip into his savings to do so, if necessary.

Dorothy Brady has introduced another concept of relative income. She found that consumption and savings were dependent on the relation of individual family income to the income level, on the average, of the city or town in which the family lived. Based upon the Bureau of Labor Statistics consumer surveys for 1917–1919 and 1934–1936, her results indicated that saving is negatively correlated with community income —that is, that saving is actually smaller in communities with higher incomes. Food and housing expenditures, however, were positively correlated, at given income brackets, with this community income.

The economic literature is full of discussion of these results and of the differences incurred by the use of cross-section and time series data. On the whole, the consumption function, when either absolute or relative income is used, tends to be too simple. Income is, of course, highly important, but we must also consider many other significant variables that influence consumers to spend or save their money.

One step in this direction is the redefinition, by Milton Friedman, of the income variable as *permanent* income. According to Friedman, one of the great difficulties in using empirical data that give only measured income is the inability to separate the permanent and transitory components of income included in measured income. He regards the difficulty in reconciling the Kuznets results from time series with those from cross-section data as due to the confusion of permanent and transitory income elements in the actual data. He proposes a system in which the *true* income variable to use in analyzing the income-spending relationship is the permanent income that an individual expects to get over the span of his working life.

This permanent income is related to the rate of interest at which the consumer can borrow or lend, the ratio of nonhuman wealth to income, and a number of transitory factors such as family size and age. In order to test his hypothesis, Friedman set up a system whereby, with current data, from which one can only secure "measured income," he believes we can separate the permanent and transitory elements.

Measured income at a particular date naturally includes both permanent and transitory income, and measured consumption also covers both permanent and transitory consumption. Both transitory income and consumption include short-run increases or decreases in income and consumption. In order to make this system operable, Friedman had to make an additional specification—that no statistical relationship exists between the transitory elements of both consumption and income or between permanent and transitory consumption or permanent and transitory income. Economists have greatly questioned the first assumption, namely, that there is no relationship between transitory consumption and transitory income.

Indeed, several authors have made empirical studies on this point, attempting to use "windfall gains" as typified by the 1950 soldiers' bonus in the United States and the Israeli bonus for 1957–1958 as transitory income. In the United States, Bodkin found that the veterans spent a higher proportion and saved less out of the windfall income than out of their basic income. Kreinin, however, came to the opposite conclusion for Israel, where the marginal propensity to consume out of the bonus was very low and out of disposable income high! This controversy is still continuing in current journals.[2]

On the whole, although Friedman has certainly contributed to consumer theory by his concept of permanent income, isolating permanent income as such from current statistical information without additional variables is no easy matter. The best statistical study so far

[2] The initial articles were: Ronald Bodkin, "Windfall Income and Consumption," *American Economic Review* (September, 1959); M. E. Kreinin, "Windfall Income and Consumption," *American Economic Review* (June, 1961).

is that of Margaret Reid, using the 1950 Bureau of Labor Statistics Consumer Expenditure Survey, in which she finds that almost none of the windfall gains went to expenditures that were not classed as consumer capital and that a great deal went to savings in the form of net assets.[3] These results tend to confirm Friedman's hypothesis and to contradict Bodkin's findings.

Consumer Preference Theory

Individual consumer preference theory may be epitomized by the contribution of John Hicks. In 1939 he brought together in one volume the ideas of his predecessors, such as Alfred Marshall, Vilfredo Pareto, and Eugenio Slutsky, and formulated a consistent theoretical structure.

In the first place, he threw out the concept of utility, greatly revered up to that time as "explaining" consumer spending decisions. We may think of "utility" as the welfare or subjective satisfaction one receives from the purchase of a consumer good. Alfred Marshall, for example, believed that utility could be measured in cardinal terms, that is, one could say by how much he preferred one good to another. Present theorists reject this; they think that we can only say that we *prefer* an egg to coffee, but not that the utility of an additional egg is twice or three times as much to us as

[3] Margaret Reid, "Consumption, Savings and Windfall Gains," *American Economic Review* (September, 1962).

that of the last pound of coffee purchased. Rather, economists now assume that each consumer has a preference scale that enables him to *rank* his preferences in order, that is, he prefers eggs to coffee, and coffee to tea. From this we can see that he must also prefer eggs to tea.

Hicks concentrated on a concept he termed the "indifference curve." In a simplified case in which the consumer's choice is limited to two commodities, the indifference curve measures the quantity of consumer good Y that would just compensate the purchaser for the loss of an additional unit of consumer good X. Thus, for example, the indifference curve tells us how many pounds of coffee an individual would be willing to give up in order to acquire a given additional quantity of eggs—and vice versa (income remaining constant). This definition is free from any taint of utility, and Hicks calls it the marginal rate of substitution of X for Y. At the equilibrium point, then, the consumer's marginal rate of substitution is equal to the ratio of the prices of the two goods in question. If coffee costs $1 a pound and eggs 75 cents a dozen, this suggests that consumers derive equal satisfaction from one pound of coffee and sixteen eggs, and are "indifferent" as to which they choose.

Hicks dealt separately, for the two-commodity case, X and Y, with the effects of changes in income and price, and then combined the two.

In the case of changes in income, the consumer will

buy more or less of *both* X and Y, although he may increase his outlays on one faster than on the other.

If, on the other hand, the price of X should decline, with income constant and the price of Y remaining the same, the consumer will buy *more* of X and the *same* amount of Y as previously.

If we now combine these two effects, of price and income, we can see that their relative importance is greatly influenced by the size of the amount that the consumer spends on any given commodity. Thus, if X is large, the income effect is important; if X is small, the primary effect is that the consumer will substitute X for other commodities as his income rises.

For example, if X, let us say, represents expenditure on an automobile, and its price goes down, the consumer will tend to spend more on automobiles and also on other smaller budgetary items that are represented by Y, such as soap and fruits. This is an income effect.[4] If, however, X is tea, and its price declines, he may substitute tea for coffee for the time being, but his other expenditures will not change.

Marshall assumed that any one commodity would always be a relatively small proportion of the consumer's budget; hence, he neglected the income effect as of little importance. Hicks, however, did not make this

[4] A change in price on an item comprising a significant portion of the consumer's budget is, in fact, the same thing as a change in his total disposable income—it affects his ability to buy many other items in his budget.

assumption, and, from this two-commodity simplification, he developed a general equilibrium system for the economy as a whole.

Household Decision-making

The household decision-making "school" adopts the household as the basic unit of consumption. It is concerned not only with economic variables, but with many others—demographic, sociological, and psychological. It tries to measure, largely from cross-section data, the effect of such variables, as well as their interaction, one with the other, in the household decision-making process. The end result is the purchase of consumer goods and the provision for saving for the household as a whole.

The Survey Research Center, at The University of Michigan, is one of the best-known centers for such an analysis of consumer behavior. Their particular interest lies in the determination of the variables that stimulate households to buy consumer durables, houses, and net assets. Their data consist of a series of sample cross-section surveys for the United States, 1947 to date. This is one of the few time series of cross-section data available in the consumption area outside of the government, but it is not suitable for general use, since it does not disaggregate consumer expenditures, except for durable goods.

Members of this school have attempted to base their

conclusions on consumer preference theory and to extend its analysis to household or family decision-making as well as to individual decision-making. Martin David, for instance, started out to derive the household preference function, in the sense in which Hicks did for the individual, from the preference functions of individuals. He finally abandoned this attempt, in a theoretical sense, because he found that individual preferences were, in fact, superseded by a family preference when it came to the actual decision to buy. This family preference may, indeed, turn out to be quite different from the individual preferences of family members. He came to the conclusion, however, that family composition at a particular point in time largely determines the household preference function.

Household decisions as to what to buy differ over time, even though a customary long-run level of living for the family over the life-cycle has been established, in accordance with family composition. The age, sex, marital status, expectations, and planning horizons of the family at any one time are important. But David then set out to determine family preference orderings indirectly by examining the effects of family composition on consumer buying behavior. He suggests, also, that established consumption and savings patterns are not easily changed, even if family size, age structure, and other variables change. There will be a lag in buying behavior.

If family size does increase, David makes the following hypotheses: (1) The family will buy commodities at quantity rates (the "family-size" items), that is, *small* families will tend to purchase certain goods at higher prices than large families; (2) large families will substitute home-produced services (such as eating at home more often than going to restaurants, having their own washing machines, and so on) for commercially produced services; (3) where quality can be measured by average price, increasing family size will be associated with the consumption of lower-*quality* goods.

In other words, with income constant, the family of increasing size will make the larger expenditures necessitated by buying lower-priced goods, by buying goods at quantity rates, and by substituting home for commercial services. Home services do not cost anything except the time of household members. David went on to test these and other hypotheses from empirical data. In his analysis, David sticks rather closely to economic factors, although recognizing the existence of the sociological and psychological variables which lie behind the household decision-making process.

This is not the case for the majority of those who contributed to the fourth Conference of Consumer Behavior, Inc.[5] Except for Hendrik Houthakker, Vernon Lippitt, and a few others, the papers deal with family

[5] In Nelson N. Foote, ed., *Household Decision-Making* (New York: New York University Press, 1961). The papers and discussions referred to above and in the next few pages are taken from this volume.

decision-making on the basis of "interpersonal relationships," as determined by sociological and psychological
factors, their interaction on individual personalities
and, therefore, upon their decision to buy, or not to
buy, certain goods.

Take, for example, James Morgan's "A Model for Individual Decisions," in which individual preferences
for Alternative A and Alternative B are compared (see
Chart 1). The individual preference for Alternative A
is based on (1) the physical and sociopsychological needs
of the person, (2) the incentive values of the expected
outcome of A for each need, and (3) his expectation as
to what the outcome will be. These factors are balanced
by inertia, which must be taken into account in determining the degree of preference for A. A similar analysis of the strength of preference for Alternative B takes
place, in which the expected satisfaction from B provides some resistance to the preference for A. The decision to buy A or B depends, then, on the extent to
which all these factors influencing the choice dominate
the strength of the preference for A as compared with
that for B. Although such physical, sociological, and
psychological variables certainly lie behind individual
consumer decisions as to what to buy in the market
place, the question might well be asked as to whether
it is the economist's job to tackle this kind of analysis.

Vernon Lippitt pointed this out in his discussion of
the Houthakker and Kenkel papers. Houthakker's system of analysis may be classified as purely economic in
nature. He starts with economic variables such as in-

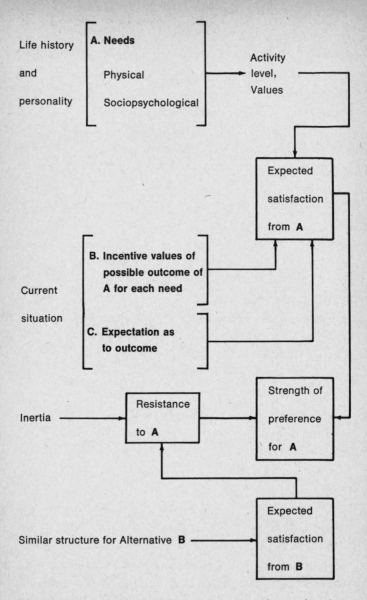

CHART 1 / *Individual Preference for Alternative* A

SOURCE: Adapted from James N. Morgan, "A Model for Individual Decisions," in Nelson N. Foote, ed., *Household Decision-Making* (New York: New York University Press, 1961), p. 88.

come, price, stocks, savings, and credit as his inputs, which, in turn, react upon the consumer units (either individual or aggregate) by influencing their decision as to what consumer goods they will buy. This is an objective analysis; there is no attempt to examine the effect of underlying social or psychological factors upon the decision-making process itself.

Kenkel, on the other hand, is primarily concerned with those sociological and psychological elements that induce the decision-making by either the husband or the wife. He pays little attention to the outputs and actual buying behavior. He is interested primarily in the inputs and the resulting system: who makes the decision, husband or wife, and the sociological factors that determine the choice of the decision-maker.

A relationship exists among the three phases of the theoretical analysis of consumer behavior that we have covered. One might look upon the consumption function in its various forms as an attempt to deal with the income effect of consumer preference theory—that is, the manner in which income changes influence changes in the size and composition of consumer spending decisions.

The difficulty is in deciding what kind of income we are going to use. We have seen that there are, currently, three definitions of what income is. Absolute income is the easiest to deal with, as it can be taken from current statistical data.

For both relative and permanent income, the problem is more difficult. Relative income can be approximated by taking the relationship between the consumers' current and previous peak incomes (or consumption)—a more complicated process, but it has been done. The measurement of permanent income, which includes many other variables, has not really been solved as yet, although there is a great deal of essential wisdom in the concept. And economists are still unwilling to swallow the assumption that there is no relationship between transitory income and consumption.

Nevertheless, it seems clear that "income" needs to be considered as more than just absolute income. If some form of relative or permanent income is used in determining the consumption function, it might be asked whether this is not one way of introducing as well many of the noneconomic variables that we have discussed as influencing consumers to buy the goods they do.

Economists would certainly like to derive household preference schedules from the schedules of individual family members, but this has not yet been done. David comes nearest to it, in concept, and Morgan sees the possibility. Can it be done without including a great many noneconomic variables? They affect the individual preference schedules, and the process by which decisions emerge and lead to actual consumer behavior in the market place.

Fundamentally, the Hicksian analysis still stands and contributes both to the consumption function advocates and to the decision-making school. Utility itself, however, as a fundamental concept, has vanished, re-placed by the marginal rate of substitution of one good for another, under the conditions postulated by Hicks.

CHAPTER 3

The Measurement of Consumption

Cross-section studies of consumer expenditures and income, in which consumer expenditures are ranked by income class, began in 1888 in the United States, when Carroll Wright became the first commissioner of labor statistics in the new Department of Labor. The aim of the early studies was to relate workers' consumer expenditures and incomes to production costs and competitive conditions in various industries that specialized in international trade. These were not unlike the eighteenth-century budget studies in England, in which the effect of wages on export prices was also subject to scrutiny. It was, indeed, a form of mercantilism.

However, in 1917–1919, after World War I, one of the first large-scale studies of consumer expenditures and incomes was conducted by the Bureau of Labor Statistics and the War Labor Board. Their main purpose was then, as today, to obtain weights for the cost-of-living index. An analysis of the results seems to confirm Engel's laws. The percentage of food bought decreased with income; the percentage for clothing increased; the percentage for rent, fuel, and light decreased; the percentage for furniture increased "up to a certain point"; and the percentage for miscellaneous (including movies, doctors, hospital bills, and everything else) increased, but not regularly.

The next large-scale study came in 1935–1936, at the height of the Great Depression. This survey was a Works Progress Administration project, coordinated by the National Resources Planning Board, which prepared the final reports. The Bureau of Labor Statistics conducted the survey in selected cities while the Bureau of Home Economics did a similar survey for small cities, villages, and rural areas.

The initial sample for incomes was extremely large (700,000), although the sample finally used consisted of 300,000 families and a small sample of single individuals. Income here was not defined as disposable income, since it included income and other taxes; however, as taxes were then very low, this does not matter greatly for comparative purposes. The sample used for consumer expenditures was smaller, consisting of 42,000 families covering 51 cities, 140 villages, and 66 farm counties.

The main purpose of this survey, apart from supplying weights for the cost-of-living index, was a study of living conditions as a basis for economic policy in the depression. What was to be done about "one-third of a nation," the poverty class?

Since that time there have been three major studies, all conducted by the Bureau of Labor Statistics and/or the United States Department of Agriculture. The first was that for 1941, *Family Spending and Saving in Wartime,* based on 3,100 families. The second took place in 1950, covered the urban population, and was based on 12,489 families. The third was the survey of 1960–1961, with samples of 4,700 families for cities and of 5,000 for rural farm and nonfarm families. Over the whole period, both the Bureau of Labor Statistics and the United States Department of Agriculture conducted special studies of their own on individual cities, rural areas, and so on.

Obviously, there are a large number of these sample studies, prepared by the federal government, from which some estimate of the changes in consumer expenditures and income over the years can be made. However, they are not all completely comparable; furthermore, the latest studies use much smaller samples, as a result of improvements in sampling techniques.

This is not all. There are, outside of the government: The University of Michigan Survey Research Center cross-section sample (mentioned previously); the *Life* Survey of 1956—a marketing survey carried out by Alfred Politz Research, Inc.; and many individual city studies for occupational groups, relief families, and other small segments of the population.

As we are unable to cover all of these studies here,

for our purposes we shall emphasize the study for 1935–1936, the 1941 survey, and the two post-World War II surveys for 1950 and 1960–1961.

Consumption in 1935–1936

This study was undertaken by the Works Progress Administration in Washington, D.C. The results of the 1935–1936 survey were published in two parts: the first dealing with income and the second with consumer expenditures. In both, the population was divided into three groups: the lower, the middle, and the upper thirds. The lower third included a larger portion of families receiving public assistance and living on farms, and a smaller number in professional, business, and clerical occupations. The share of average total income held by the lower third was about 10 percent, with an average income of $471 per family.

The middle-income group received 24 percent of aggregate income and had an average income of $1076. The upper third secured 66 percent of aggregate income with an average income per family of $3000. This figure was based on an extremely wide income range, including incomes from $1450 to those of over $1,000,000. This group also had larger families. The majority lived in large cities, and 80 percent were not receiving public assistance.[1] Over 60 percent were from the business and clerical groups.

[1] In the expenditure survey, families on public assistance in which *both* husband and wife were foreign born were excluded.

If one contrasts the percentage of total expenditures on consumer goods accounted for by the lower and upper thirds, the picture is as given by Table 1.

TABLE 1 / Percentage of Total Consumption of Selected Goods and Services Accounted for by Highest- and Lowest-income Classes

	Lower Third	Upper Third
Food	20	50
Housing	16	60
Household operation	13	60
Clothing	11	64
Recreation	8	71
Automobile	5	75

It is not surprising that the survey report emphasized the dominance of the upper third in the market for consumer goods since, with the exception of food, they accounted for over 50 percent of total expenditures for each of the main items, with 71 and 75 percent, respectively, for recreation and automobiles. The report found as well that expenditures for automobiles and recreation rose most rapidly, both absolutely and proportionately, with income.

The summary volumes of the 1935–1936 study read rather like a religious tract—or political propaganda.[2] Every effort was made to contrast the extremes of pov-

[2] *Consumer Incomes in the United States* and *Consumer Expenditures in the United States,* National Resources Committee (Washington, D.C., 1938 and 1939, respectively).

erty and riches that were found to exist. The survey, however, was as carefully done as statistical techniques of the time allowed—and any biases in the data are probably due to the inadequacies of available techniques.

Certainly the situation in 1935–1936 *was* disastrous. Some 25 percent of the labor force was unemployed; apple sellers, bread lines, the march of the unemployed to Washington—all emphasized this fact. However, the depression only served to intensify an inequality of the income and expenditure distributions that already existed in the twenties but was not generally realized (see Chapter 5).

The results of the 1935–1936 survey were well publicized. They affected public consciousness and the government programs. President Roosevelt went on the radio to talk about the "ill-fed," the "ill-clothed," and the "ill-housed" third. A new social philosophy began to appear, a kind of social conscience that upheld the idea that society cannot allow its citizens to starve, or even to fall below some minimum standard of welfare. It was suggested that responsibility lay with the government to take over this task; in a highly industrialized society an individualistic philosophy is no longer adequate. This was a precursor to the current "war on poverty."

As a matter of fact, the government did take over many of these responsibilities. Straight relief measures (Works Progress Administration, Civilian Conservation Corps, and so on), as well as social security and unemployment insurance, resulted from the implementation of this philosophy in the thirties. Perhaps of greatest long-run importance was the National Employment Act of 1946, which set up the Council of Economic Advisers and gave the President responsibility to maintain maximum employment.

Consumer Expenditures and Income in 1941, 1950, and 1960–1961

Let us now turn to the three latest consumer expenditure surveys and subject them to comparison, insofar as possible. The 1941 and 1960–1961 surveys are based upon samples of the total population of the United States. The 1950 study, however, included only the urban population, so that in this case, the comparison will be made with the urban part of the 1960–1961 survey.

We begin with the main aspects of the 1960–1961 study and work backward from there. Table 2 shows some of the key characteristics of the sample of families and individuals included in the survey.

As might be expected, total expenditures and money income for farm and nonfarm families are successively lower in absolute amount than those for urban families. In other money receipts and net change in assets and liabilities, however, farm families are the highest. Both nonfarm and farm families have larger families and a considerably higher percentage own their own homes and cars. The percentage of nonwhite families

TABLE 2 / Key Characteristics, 1960–1961 Survey
(average per family)

	Total	Urban	Nonfarm	Farm
(DOLLARS)				
Total expenditures	5047	5390	4296	3594
Money income before taxes	6246	6691	5168	4732
Money income after taxes	5557	5906	4700	4424
Other money receipts	81	82	76	98
Net change in assets and liabilities[a]	+199	+177	+176	+519
(PERCENT)				
Nonwhite	11	12	6	8
Home owners	57	53	67	71
Auto owners	76	73	82	91

NOTE: Average family size: total, 3.2; urban, 3.1; nonfarm, 3.5; farm, 3.8.

[a] Net changes in assets and liabilities are the algebraic sum of increases and decreases in assets and liabilities. Net increases in assets or decreases in liabilities represent a net saving (+) during the year. Net decreases in assets or increases in liabilities represent a deficit (−) or net dissaving.

SOURCE: *Consumer Expenditures and Income, Total United States, Urban and Rural, 1960–61* (Washington, D.C.: Bureau of Labor Statistics Report No. 237–93, U.S. Department of Agriculture Report CES–15, 1965), p. 2.

in cities is almost double the percentage in farm and nonfarm areas.

Table 3 lists the percentages of total expenditures that go to various items of consumption. Urban consumers spend a higher percentage on alcohol, housing, recreation, reading and education, and other transport

TABLE 3 / Percentage of Total Expenditures for Current Consumption, 1960–1961 Survey

	Total	Urban	Nonfarm	Farm
Food	24.5	24.3	25.2	24.1
Tobacco	1.8	1.8	2.0	1.8
Alcohol	1.5	1.7	1.2	0.8
Housing (total)	28.9	29.5	27.7	25.5
Clothing	10.3	10.4	9.5	11.9
Personal care	2.9	2.9	2.9	2.9
Medical care	6.7	6.6	6.9	8.6
Recreation	4.0	4.0	3.8	3.4
Reading and education	1.9	2.0	1.6	1.8
Automobile	13.7	13.0	16.3	16.4
Other transport	1.5	1.7	0.9	0.7
Other expenditures	2.2	2.2	2.1	2.1

SOURCE: *Consumer Expenditures and Income, Total United States, Urban and Rural, 1960–61* (Washington, D.C.: Bureau of Labor Statistics Report No. 237–93, U.S. Department of Agriculture Report CES–15, 1965), p. 2.

(all transport except automobiles). Nonfarm families spend a greater percentage on food and tobacco and the least of the three groups on clothing and reading and education. Farm families have lower percentage expenditures for food, alcohol, housing, recreation, and other transport. Both farm and nonfarm families spend considerably more on automobiles than urban families spend. The percentage for personal care is the same for all three types of families.

Comparison of 1960–1961 Survey with 1940–1941 Survey[3]

When we compare the 1960–1961 survey with that for 1941, we find a considerable difference between these years in expenditure and income per family. In 1941 total expenditures per family averaged $1666 as compared with the 1960–1961 figure of $5047; and annual money income was $1948 as contrasted with $5557. Income and other taxes were only $26 per family in 1941, but had risen to $689 by 1960–1961.

During this twenty-year period, urban families increased from 62 to 75 percent of the population. Levels of expenditure for rural nonfarm and farm families were lower than those for urban families in both studies, but by 1960–1961 the national pattern of income and spending had more nearly approached that of the urban families, as a result of rapidly increasing urbanization.

Nonfarm families in metropolitan areas averaged higher incomes and expenditures than urban families in 1960–1961, although they made up only 27 percent of the rural nonfarm group. These families probably represent the higher-income groups who have moved to the suburbs since World War II.

For the group as a whole (urban, rural nonfarm, and

[3] *Consumer Expenditures and Income, Total United States, Urban and Rural, 1960–61* (Washington, D.C.: Bureau of Labor Statistics Report No. 237–93, U.S. Department of Agriculture Report CES–15, 1965).

farm), after-tax income rose 41 percent and expenditures 50 percent from 1941 to 1960–1961, even *when the figures are adjusted for price changes.* Of course, it must be remembered that in 1941 the depression of the thirties was not entirely over. It took World War II to accomplish its demise.

Urban Consumer Expenditures and Incomes in 1950 and 1960–1961

The urban part of the consumer purchases study for 1960–1961 may be compared with the study for 1950, which did not include rural nonfarm and farm families. The data in Table 4 give some idea of the principal changes in family characteristics during the period.

After correction for price changes during the ten-year period, after-tax income increased by 22 percent and total expenditures by 14 percent. Net change in assets and liabilities rose from a negative amount in 1950 to a plus $177 in 1960–1961. The proportion of nonwhite families rose 2 percentage points; of home owners, 5 percentage points; and of automobile owners, 14 percentage points. Average family size changed very little, although a much greater variation appears in the individual city figures.

The percentages of expenditures for current consumption in the two years are shown in Table 5.

For the first time, it is notable that the percentage spent on food has relinquished first place to the percentage spent on the housing complex. In all previous

TABLE 4 / Changes in Characteristics of Urban Families,
1950 and 1960–1961
(*average per family*)

	1950	1960–1961
(DOLLARS)		
Total expenditures	3808	5390
Money income before taxes	4237	6691
Money income after taxes	3910	5906
Other money receipts	49	82
Net change in assets and liabilities[a]	−74	+177
(PERCENT)		
Nonwhite	10	12
Home owners	48	53
Auto owners	59	73

NOTE: Number of families in sample: 1960–1961, 9,476; 1950, 12,489.
Average family size: 1960–1961, 3.1; 1950, 3.0.

[a] Net changes in assets and liabilities are the algebraic sum of increases
and decreases in assets and liabilities. Net increases in assets or decreases in liabilities represent a net saving (+) during the year. Net
decreases in assets or increases in liabilities represent a deficit (−) or
net dissaving.

SOURCE: *Consumer Expenditures and Income, Urban United States,
1960–61* (Washington, D.C.: Bureau of Labor Statistics Report No.
237–38, 1964), p. 2.

studies, the highest proportion spent has gone for food.
The percentage spent on clothing has decreased and,
also, that for recreation and other transport. The decline in recreation may, in part, be explained by the
fact that meals and recreational expenditures connected
with automobile use are included under automobile
expenditures and not under those for recreation. The

TABLE 5 / Percentage of Expenditures for Current Consumption by Urban Families, 1950 and 1960–1961

	1950	1960–1961
Food	29.7	24.3
Tobacco	1.8	1.8
Alcohol	1.7	1.7
Housing (total)	27.2	29.5
Clothing	11.5	10.4
Personal care	2.2	2.9
Medical care	5.2	6.6
Recreation	4.4	4.0
Reading and education	1.5	2.0
Automobile	11.6	13.0
Other transport	1.8	1.7
Other expenditures	1.4	2.2

SOURCE: *Consumer Expenditures and Income, Urban United States, 1960–61* (Washington, D.C.: Bureau of Labor Statistics Report No. 237–38, 1964), p. 2.

percentage for automobile use has gone up. If one takes food, clothing, and housing together, their combined share of total expenditures dropped from 57 percent to 53 percent over the decade. This is largely a result of the increasing percentage spent on automobiles, medical care, and education.

It is only possible to summarize here what has happened to consumption in the United States over the years. Since the depression of the thirties there has been a steady increase in both consumer expenditures and income. For the whole sample, incomes have in-

creased 41 percent and expenditures 50 percent between 1941 and 1960–1961. In comparing the urban
sections between 1950 and 1960–1961, incomes rose by
22 percent and expenditures by 14 percent. It appears
that the greater percentage increase in both income
and expenditures came during and immediately after
World War II.

However, since the war period itself is not typical,
it seems best to rely upon the urban comparisons between 1950 and 1960–1961. Since the United States is
becoming more and more urbanized, and the agricultural sector is declining, this is not an unrepresentative
procedure.

We appear to be a nation that spends nearly 29 percent of our total expenditures for the elements of housing, including household operation, furnishings, and
equipment. Some 25 percent goes for food, and the
next highest item is nearly 14 percent for automobile
purchase and operation. While 57 percent of the representative sample of the population are home owners,
76 percent are owners of automobiles. Clothing expenditures rank next, slightly over 10 percent; and
medical care and recreation follow, in that order.

Is this preponderance of car and home owners also
typical of other countries? In the U.S.S.R., at present,
the proportion of consumers who are home and car
owners is not high, although homes and cars are, perhaps, the two major durable goods that the people most
want. In 1964, the Russian stock of cars permitted one
car for every 250 persons, as compared to one car for

fewer than three people in the United States. Despite very high prices, hundreds in Moscow signed the re-opened waiting lists for car purchases in 1963. There is also a waiting list for good refrigerators, although some other durables, such as transistor radios, are in better supply.[4] The quality of durable goods in Russia is being improved, and now both refrigerators and tele-vision sets are appearing in greater supply in city stores.[5]

Kuznets has made a comparison of the percentage distribution of private consumption expenditures of eight European countries with those of the United States for 1950.[6] In examining certain key items—food, clothing, total housing, and private transport—very marked differences appear. The countries included in this comparative study are Belgium, the United King-dom, Denmark, Norway, France, Germany, the Nether-lands, and Italy. In all cases, except possibly for total housing, the percentage spent in the eight European countries was very different from that spent in the United States.

The percentage spent for food in the United States

[4] David W. Bronson and Barbara S. Severin, "Recent Trends in Consumption and Disposable Money Income in the U.S.S.R.," *New Directions in the Soviet Economy,* Studies Prepared for the Subcommittee on Foreign Policy, Joint Economic Committee, 89th Congress of the United States, 2nd Session, 1966, Section 4.

[5] *The New York Times,* October 30, 1966.

[6] "Quantitative Aspects of the Economic Growth of Nations: The Share and Structure of Consumption," *Economic Development and Cultural Change,* Vol. X, No. 2 (January, 1962). The percentage figures used here are in terms of domestic prices.

was 24.1. All of the eight countries were above this figure, with France and Germany 36 and 38 percent, respectively. Italy topped the list with nearly 50 percent of its total consumption going for food. For total housing,[7] the discrepancy was not as great, although the European figures were consistently somewhat lower than the 24.8 percent spent in the United States, except in the case of Italy, where housing expenditure was only 9.8 percent.

For private transport the United States figure was 10.5 percent, very much higher than in any of these European countries, where the figures ranged from 3.2 percent for Belgium down to 1.2 percent in Norway. The percentage spent for clothing was consistently higher in Europe. The 11 percent figure for the United States was exceeded by the lowest European figures, 12.4 and 12.8 percent for the United Kingdom and France; and especially by the over 16 percent level exhibited by Denmark, Norway, the Netherlands, and Italy.

The European Scientific Association for Medium and Long-Term Forecasting (ASEPELT) figures for 1960 and forecasts for 1970, for Belgium, France, Italy, the Netherlands, Norway, and Sweden,[8] indicate the possibility that changes are occurring. The percentages

---

[7] The figure includes four subtotals: housing; fuel, light, and water; household goods; and household operations.

[8] *Europe's Future Consumption* (Amsterdam: North Holland Publishing Company, 1964), p. 10. These figures are in *dollars per capita* (at 1960 prices) and are not strictly comparable.

spent for food are continually going down; for durables there is a slight increase; and for transport equipment and operation, there is a definite increase. The percentages spent for clothing are quite similar in the two years.

It does not appear that the Western Europeans, any more than the Russians, have as yet attained the predominant ownership of cars and houses that is now characteristic of the United States. However, it is difficult to make these comparisons from the available figures, and the structure of European regulations concerning housing and other consumer durables is quite different from ours. It is clear, however, that their expenditures are changing, with food expenditures declining as a proportion of the total so that they are in a better position to acquire whatever durable goods are provided.

The typical American, then, is an automobile owner and a home owner. He is therefore more susceptible to the purchase of those durable goods that the possession of a home and a car entails. His expenditures on food are rising much more slowly, and he is spending more on medical care, reading, and education.

This pattern of change in expenditures (since 1950) has some relation to the increase in "leisure" time discussed in the next chapter. With a greater time "away from work" our typical American is electing to have a car and a home, in part, for his leisure hours.

CHAPTER 4

Leisure as a Consumer Good

Leisure may be looked upon both as a part of national income and as a consumer good. A number of unmeasurable elements contribute to the "income" of an individual in addition to the income he has in real money terms. Such qualitative elements might add up to a sizable amount for the economy as a whole, if it were possible to measure them. Liking one's job and many other psychological satisfactions—and dissatisfactions —might be considered as a part of national income. Although unmeasurable now in quantitative terms, such elements certainly affect and are an addition to— or subtraction from—the real output of an economic system.

Leisure, which may be defined as time away from work, is such an economic good. How this time is spent is important for the individual, the family, and the economy and can contribute to satisfaction just as much as something purchased, such as a dish of ice cream or a new dress. In the past hundred-odd years, the average work week in all industries has declined by 31.2 hours; in agriculture, by 28.2 hours; and in nonagricultural industries, by 27.7 hours. These figures are often used to show the extent to which leisure time has been increasing for the labor force, the majority of the population.

Consumer preference theory can be used to apply to the choice of leisure as compared with additional income. Indeed, the "backward-bending" supply curve for labor has been developed to indicate that there may be a point at which workers will choose to enjoy more leisure rather than more income. This supply curve relates hours of work to income received. Normally, people will be willing to work longer to earn more. However, there may be a point at which they will prefer fewer hours of work to more income, because the individual wishes to have more free time rather than a greater income.[1]

Finnegan attacks this problem statistically.[2] He sets out to test the theory that a worker will divide his time between work and leisure so as to bring to its highest point his utility or welfare. If leisure is considered a

[1] For the derelict outcasts of society—the "bums"—the desire for leisure is so great that they are content to live at extraordinarily low levels of comfort; for most of us, the desire to earn more is perhaps too strong and drives us to work too much and play too little.

[2] T. Aldrich Finnegan, "Hours of Work in the United States —A Cross-Sectional Analysis," *Journal of Political Economy* (October, 1962).

"normal" consumer good, then a permanent rise in the wage rate will produce an income effect and a substitution effect. The income effect, on the normal good assumption, would tend to shorten the work week, as the individual would prefer more leisure; the substitution effect would tend to increase the work week, since each hour of leisure would cost more in terms of what the individual *could* earn.

Since rising wage rates and decreasing overtime work have, in fact, occurred, Finnegan suggests that the income effect, rather than the substitution effect, predominates. Using 1950 cross-section data from the Census of Housing, he proceeds to test this hypothesis. Although he does come out with a negative relationship between the earnings of adult males and their hours of work, the correlation coefficient is low and a great deal of the statistical relationship is unexplained, despite his attempts to introduce many other variables. His statistical test is not a complete success. In the case of business executives, at any rate, the relationship should certainly be positive.

Whether individuals *choose* jobs with fewer hours and more pay is difficult to prove. Is it quite the same thing to hold that since certain industries have shorter work weeks, with higher pay, this is representative of consumer choice? The shorter working hours might rather be explained by technological change, union contracts, and many other factors in the economy. The usual supply curve for labor, showing the number of hours people are willing to work relative to the incomes they can earn, would be expected to rise steadily as wages and salaries increase, but the opposite hypothesis may ultimately come into play, due to the preference of individuals for more leisure. Certainly in many professional fields, such as medicine or law, a limit is often set as to the number of patients or clients who will be accepted.

The topic of leisure came into special prominence with the publication of Sebastian de Grazia's book *Of Time, Work and Leisure*.[3] This fascinating volume analyzes the concept of leisure and the question of whether the figures that indicate a decreasing work week can actually be used to show that an increase in leisure for the United States working force has occurred.

De Grazia does not define leisure simply as "time away from work." He considers leisure to be an active state; one must do something *not* connected with earning a living that contributes to society as a whole. He returns to the idea of leisure in Greek, Roman, and medieval times, when the leisure class was composed of poets, musicians, artists, politicians, and the like, who worked for the state or the arts—but not to earn a living.[4] Such a definition of leisure is not really applicable to a modern economy, where the average person

[3] Sebastian de Grazia, *Of Time, Work and Leisure* (New York: Twentieth Century Fund, 1962).

[4] It may be noted that in many cases they did not have to work for a living; *their* leisure was based on a slave state or a feudal society.

has to work to earn a living, whether he is a poet or a politician.

However, de Grazia attacks the figures on the decline of the work week in the past hundred years, in the attempt to show that the 31.2-hour decline of the working week does not even mean free time away from work and certainly not leisure in his sense of the word. He corrects this figure, first, by subtracting vacation time and part-time employment, emerging with a figure of 25.2 hours more away from work, on the average. How is this "free time" spent? He estimates that it is spent in "moonlighting" (or taking a subsidiary job); in traveling to work; in the machine pacing of work— a more intensive working day, shorter lunch hours, fewer rest periods; in migration to new jobs; and in work around the house—since the wife frequently is gainfully employed.

He then counts the number of hours these activities connected with work take, deducts them from the above total, and comes out with the conclusion that "free time," unrelated to work, is only a few hours (something like 2.5) more than it was a hundred years ago.

De Grazia also examines certain special groups, executive and professional workers, for example. In the sense of nonwork-oriented activities, they have almost no free time. Their recreation is frequently tied to their work requirements. Even their social, athletic, civic, and other activities are not free. They may be expected to lunch, dine, play golf, and participate in civic activities as supplements to their regular occupations. They spend a great deal of their time away from work with business associates. Yet the professional groups are in many ways closest to the old idea of leisure that de Grazia so movingly describes. These people care about their work, much of which is done for reasons beyond the mere earning of a living.

This is a brief and inadequate outline of an extraordinarily fascinating book. It must be admitted, I think, that we do not ordinarily have leisure in the sense in which de Grazia defines the word. Yet, in many ways, the average worker has benefited from the decline in the official work week.

One element de Grazia neglects is choice. The average worker can now decide how to spend his time away from his primary job. He need not live far away from work, or moonlight, or migrate to another job, etc., *unless he chooses to do so*. He has more time away from his regular job and therefore can travel to work, engage in unpaid civic activities, or "do-it-himself" around the house if he wishes.

As to moonlighting, he is free to take another job, the timing of which he can arrange at *his* convenience. Many workers do moonlight and specify the times at which they will do the job—frequently at an inconvenient hour for the householder! Recent Bureau of Labor Statistics figures indicate that nearly 4 million workers hold two or more jobs, averaging more than fifty hours a week. The number of moonlighters is, in fact, about equivalent to the number of unemployed, about 5 percent of the labor force.

Marion Clawson, in "How Much Leisure, Now and in the Future," [5] defines leisure rather differently than does de Grazia. He calls it discretionary time, time beyond the hours necessary for existence and subsistence. Existence comprises sleeping, eating, and personal hygiene; and subsistence is the time spent in working to earn an income. Clawson also terms leisure "choosing time" and makes it very clear that leisure is not idleness.

Discretionary time is comparable to the concept of discretionary income, and this is defined as the amount of income remaining after expenditures on "necessities," food, clothing, and housing. Although some haziness exists in the definition of necessities, Clawson includes as leisure "all time not spent in sleep, at work, in school, or in necessary personal chores." An individual may choose to spend his leisure in recreation of one kind or another, or to use it for self-expression in many ways. He may bask in the sun, work in the garden, or take a course in playwriting or sculpturing.

A national time budget and time division of leisure has been computed, based on the total population, each member of which had 24 hours each day, for 365 days of the year. These calculations were made for 1900 and 1950 and were forecast for the year 2000, assuming

[5] Reprint published by Resources for the Future, Inc., Washington, D.C., May, 1964.

then 300 million people in the population; the figures are shown in Table 6.

An average work week of sixty hours was assumed in 1900, of forty hours in 1950, which is approximately correct. It was forecast that the average work week would drop to twenty-eight hours by the year 2000. On this basis, according to the time budget, the increase in

TABLE 6

Uses of Times	1900	1950	2000	Percent Rise in Leisure Time, 2000 vs. 1900
	(billions of hours annually)			
Total time	667	1,329	2,907	
Sleep	265	514	1,131	
Work	86	132	206	
Schools	11	32	90	
Housekeeping	61	68	93	
Preschool, nonsleeping hours	30	56	110	
Personal care	37	74	164	
Total (above)	490	876	1,794	
Remaining, largely leisure	177	453	1,113	10.5
Daily leisure hours	72	189	375	20
Weekend leisure hours	50	179	483	10.3
Vacation	17	35	182	9.4
Retired	6	24	56	
Other	32	26	16	

SOURCE: Adapted from Mary A. Holman, "A National Time Budget for the Year 2000," *Sociology and Social Research,* Vol. 46, No. 1 (October, 1961).

total leisure time in the year 2000 would be about 10.5 percent. Daily leisure hours are expected to rise by 20 percent, weekends are increased by 13 percent more time, and vacations will rise by 9 percent.

How this work week should be arranged is of considerable significance. Clawson argues that it would be far better to have increased leisure time for weekends and vacations than, simply, shorter working days. He thinks that then additional time is more likely to be used purposefully and will not be frittered away. Yet the time budget gives the greatest increase to daily leisure hours.

Available data show that outdoor recreation has increased greatly in the past few years: camping in parks, outdoor sports, boating, fishing, and so on. Many more individuals and families now participate in cultural and sports activities—concerts, art museums, baseball games—and there has developed considerably more self-expression by individuals in such activities as dramatics, drawing, painting, and jewelry-making.

Clawson points out that people need to be educated for leisure in order to use it effectively. A lot of "un-fun" activities have been taken up out of pure boredom and as an escape from leisure or free time. Television, for instance, frequently belongs in that category. Possibly the teen-age entrance into crime and riots is a symptom of their not knowing what to do with their leisure time. It is, in any case, a vexing problem in both the United States and Great Britain. What will happen by the year 2000, with additional leisure time in the offing? Are people going to spend it engaged in escapist activities or are they going to educate and train themselves to use this extra time purposefully and for the benefit of themselves and society? Some of the major trade unions are, indeed, becoming concerned with this problem and are setting up procedures and recreational areas in which union members may be educated and trained, not only for their jobs, but for their leisure hours. In Great Britain, for example, Arnold Wesker provided traveling theater groups that gave performances in various industrial centers under trade union sponsorship.

Both de Grazia and Clawson agree that some individuals would rather utilize their "leisure" hours for their business or professional pursuits, but that these people are relatively few in the context of the general population. However, with the increase in education expected by the end of the century, it is possible that this subgroup of the population may grow and include a far higher proportion of the population than it now does.

However one defines leisure, the effective use of leisure time is a real problem now and will be even more of one in the future. Official working hours have been and are declining. This process is likely to be accelerated by longer paid vacations, the impact of technological change in industry, and new agreements reached on working hours and other conditions of employment by the major unions and large-scale industry. People will have to be taught to use these leisure hours, not only for personal pleasure, but in contributing to local and national activities, enhancing their own education, and taking up many pursuits that cannot be classified as "unfun," in Clawson's sense of the word.

CHAPTER 5

Poverty and Millionaires

Since the discussion in this chapter is based on changes in the size distribution of income over time, we should define this concept at the start. The size distribution of income is, in essence, a cross-section picture of the income distribution at any one time. Other cross-section studies have been used, and defined, in previous chapters. For our purposes, here, the income size distribution shows, for any given period of time, the percentage of families and individuals receiving an average income, by successive income classes from zero to the end of the income distribution. The comparison of such size distributions for a series of specific years will reflect changes in the shape of the distributions over time and will show whether income is being distributed more or less equally.

We can examine the range of the low- and of the high-income groups from the point of view of such size distributions of income and also by abstract measures of income inequality. Size distributions of income are more relevant to the problem of defining the size of the lower and upper ends of the income distribution, in which the poverty and very high-income groups fall. *Measures of inequality* indicate to what extent the income distribution, taken as a whole, deviates from complete equality.

There are a number of income size distributions for the United States going back to 1921. A selected sample of these charts will be examined here.[1]

Chart 2 shows the distribution of income in 1929. These figures are taken from *America's Capacity to Consume*[2] and are for all income recipients. There is also an income distribution for 1921 (not shown here). These two distributions are very much alike, except for the first point, with by far the largest number of people in the under-$2000 group, a sharp decline in the number in the $2000–$4000 category, and then a level stretch of very low numbers thereafter.

The chart also shows later distributions, put together by the late Selma Goldsmith of the Office of Business Economics,[3] which indicate a steady progres-

[1] The problems of comparability between the years, especially for the early ones, are very great. Different sources have different definitions of their samples, and these are indicated on the charts.

[2] By Maurice Leven, Harold G. Moulton, and Clark Warburton (Washington, D.C.: Brookings, 1934).

[3] Mrs. Goldsmith died shortly after her work on income distribution had been completed. The income distributions are now published regularly by the Office of Business Economics.

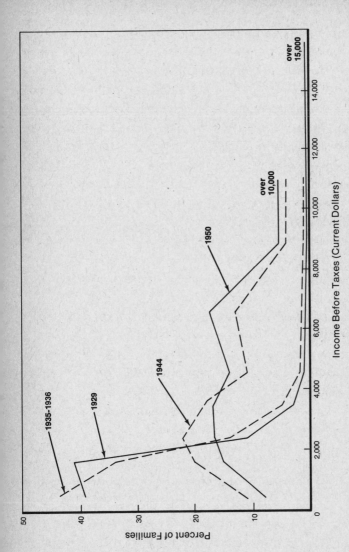

CHART 2 / *1929–1950 Distribution of Incomes in the United States*

Income Before Taxes (Current Dollars)

Percent of Families

SOURCE: Data after 1929 from Selma Goldsmith, George Jaszi, Hyman Kaitz, and Maurice Liebenberg, "Size Distribution of Income since the Mid-Thirties," *The Review of Economics and Statistics* (February, 1954).

sion in the shape of the distribution from 1935–1936 to 1950. The 1935–1936 distribution is similar in shape to the distributions for 1921 and 1929, but by 1941, there is a distinct change. The numbers below $2000 decrease, and there is a shift of the entire curve to the right. These changes are accentuated in 1944, when the peak income group shifts to *over* $2000, with a second peak over $6000. By 1950, the distribution had shifted to an even greater extent, showing equal peaks at $3000 and over $6000 and considerably more people in the higher-income groups.

By 1963, the first income group peak occurred at $6000, with a somewhat lower peak at $11,000, and with very many more income recipients than previously in the income groups above $12,000. This is for the whole sample of families. For the farm and nonwhite families, income peaks occur in the early class intervals, but their main concentration is at the $4000 level, with a precipitate decline after that, a decline that is much greater than the decrease for the population as a whole.

As one can see, the United States income distribution has remained relatively stable since the late forties. The income level for the low-income groups has risen and the number in the middle-income groups has increased. The whole distribution has, indeed, shifted upward and to the right, with the middle-income groups stretching out to cover a greater range of the population. But income is still unequally distributed. This is shown by the Lorenz curve analysis (Chart 3). Here, the percentages of income held by percentages of

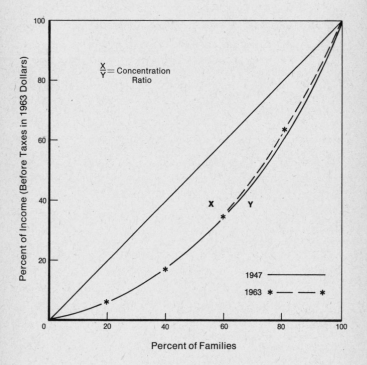

CHART 3 / *Lorenz Curves for the United States,*
1947 and 1963

SOURCE: United States Bureau of the Census, No. 43, 1964.

the population for 1947 and 1963 are plotted. If income *were* equally distributed, then 20 percent of families would receive 20 percent of income, 40 percent of families 40 percent of income, and so on up to 100 percent. Such an equality of income distribution is represented by the diagonal line in the chart. Since income was not equally distributed in either 1947 or 1963, these lines fall some distance from the diagonal line of equal distribution. In fact, the income distributions for 1947 and 1963 are very much alike, except that the upper end of the 1963 curve is slightly nearer the diagonal equality line. The extent of inequality still existing could be measured by dividing area X by area Y and, if computed, would indicate that considerable inequality still exists.

Irving Kravis has made a study of changes in inequality from 1888–1890 through 1958, using an index of inequality based on the Lorenz curve concentration ratio.[4] These indexes, which are shown in Table 7, indicate that inequality was highest in 1888–1890 and lowest in 1918. The index increased in 1935–1936, went down in 1941, and has continued at a lower level since then. However, it has never reached the 1918 figure. Kravis attributes the decline in the inequality index to a greater *relative* rise in the low-, and especially in the middle-, income groups. He feels, contrary to Kuznets,[5]

[4] Irving Kravis, *The Structure of Income* (Philadelphia: University of Pennsylvania Press, 1962).

[5] Simon Kuznets, "Economic Growth and Income Inequality," *American Economic Review* (March, 1955).

TABLE 7 / Indexes of Inequality, Selected Years,
1888–1958
(*1950 = 100*)

1888–1890	137
1901	95
1918	89
1935–1936	116
1941	110
1944	98
1950	100
1956	97
1958	98

SOURCE: Adapted from Irving Kravis, *The Structure of Income* (Philadelphia: University of Pennsylvania Press, 1962), p. 213.

that a decline in property shares, which are now widely held by the middle-, as well as by the top-income groups, played only a "modest" role.

Poverty

Although the income distribution has risen in level and shifted and stretched itself to the right, where the middle-income groups are predominant, its relative stability since the late forties is really quite remarkable. The low-income peak is no longer below $2000, but in 1963 had risen to $6000; the middle-income groups cover a much larger range of incomes than they used to do, and the upper tail of the distribution has also lengthened. Nevertheless, relative poverty still exists, and incomes are still unequal. The "poor" are still with us, although their poverty is at a considerably higher level than in the past. Today, in the United States, this poverty group is defined as those who have incomes below $3100.[6]

The United States government has now set up a program that attempts to mitigate, with the hope that it may eventually abolish, poverty. In 1964, the Economic Opportunity Act was passed and, according to the Council of Economic Advisers, "marked the opening of an enlarged attack on inadequate incomes in an economy of relative abundance. The main thrust of this effort is directed at the roots of poverty—particularly at helping the children of the poor." [7] The Office of Economic Opportunity was established to offer education, training, and work experience to youth, and to coordinate other government programs dealing less overtly with poverty. A budget of $1.5 billion was allocated to the Office of Economic Opportunity for this purpose.

Since *Income and Welfare in the United States*[8] had considerable influence on the government program, it will be examined here briefly. The authors undertake to answer questions such as these: How can the poverty group be estimated? Will economic growth take care of

[6] See Walter Galenson, *A Primer on Employment and Wages* (New York: Random House, 1966); David Hamilton, *A Primer on Poverty* (New York: Random House, in preparation).

[7] *Economic Report of the President,* January, 1965.

[8] James N. Morgan, Martin H. David, Wilbur J. Cohen, and Harvey E. Brazer, *Income and Welfare in the United States* (New York: McGraw-Hill, 1962). This study was conducted by the Survey Research Center of The University of Michigan.

the problem? Can the government do it? Will there always be a poverty group resulting from the mental,
physical, and psychological differences in human be-
ings?

Morgan and his associates undertake a very detailed
study of family and individual incomes. They analyze
the importance of a series of variables on the determination of the level of income for a number of income
groups, and how such levels change. Among all these
variables, they find that *formal education* is by far the
most important for its effect on both the husband and
the wife.

In Part III, which is specifically on poverty, they emphasize the following points:

(1) Poverty has declined in the United States and
other highly developed countries, including Russia, despite differences in their political and economic systems.

(2) Economic growth per se does not eliminate poverty. General programs of education, income and
health measures, tax systems, and an optimum use of
resources are needed.

(3) The United States could, today, eliminate the
poverty of families and individuals living on incomes
that are now below subsistence level at a cost of $10
billion a year. This is less than 2 percent of gross national product, 10 percent of tax revenues, and one-
fifth the cost of national defense.

(4) The most significant factor among the causes of
poverty is the lack of *formal education,* since formal
education is "the major dynamic mechanism by which

economic level is passed on from one generation to the next, or by which *intergenerational change takes place*." [9]

(5) In attempting to evaluate welfare from the income distribution, leisure should be considered. Morgan finds (as did de Grazia) that families with higher incomes work more hours. If this is involuntary, the inequality-of-income measure tends to exaggerate the inequality of welfare. These families have less leisure and are therefore less well off.[10]

The Council of Economic Advisers tends to take the view that economic growth will not cure poverty, although poverty is decreasing slowly over time. (The poverty group declined from 13.4 million in 1959 to 11.9 million in 1964, or from 24 to 19.8 percent.) They believe that it is the government's job to assist in eliminating this group, particularly as certain components of the group do not share in the slow but continual decrease. Among these are poor, single individuals; families with five or more children; families headed by females; and poor nonwhite families. In general, poverty is much greater among nonwhites, the aged, and white families headed by females.

The federal program is now being combined with state and municipal programs, area programs, educational programs, and programs initiated by other fed-

[9] *Ibid.,* p. 9.
[10] Actually, in many cases, these higher-income families *choose* to work longer hours, to combine work activity with leisure. Their lack of leisure is often voluntary. See Chapter 4.

eral agencies. It is to be noted that great stress is being put on formal education, as was advised by Morgan and his coauthors.

The Upper-income Groups

At the same time that the poverty group is decreasing, the upper end of the income distribution is rising. Also, the number of millionaires is increasing and although their wealth is not income in the technical sense, they have accumulated very large assets; for the most part in capital stocks, real estate, and tax-free state and municipal bonds.

In the last chapter of *Rich Man Poor Man*[11] Herman Miller undertakes to forecast what will happen to income and employment in 1980 and 1975. Assuming that there will be 75 million families and individuals and an aggregate income (in 1960 dollars) of 837 billion dollars in 1980, he finds that the average income of these families and individuals will be $11,200, as compared with $6800 in 1960. There will also be a considerable change in the income distribution. Those with incomes under $3000 will drop to 12 percent (from 21 percent in 1962). Those with incomes above $10,000 will rise from 19 percent of the families and individuals to 30 percent by 1980. All this assumes no inflation.

[11] New York: Crowell-Collier, 1964; and "Millionaires Are a Dime a Dozen," *The New York Times Magazine,* November 28, 1965.

By 1975, the number of workers will have risen to 93 million, with emphasis on professional and managerial workers, clerical and sales workers, craftsmen, and service workers. The number of laborers, farmers, and farm and semiskilled workers is expected to decrease. Although there are some who do not expect unemployment to increase, Miller is not one of them. He thinks that to the unskilled and semiskilled youth, Negroes, housewives, etc., who make up a large portion of the unemployed, there will be added many white-collar workers who will be replaced by automation. From 1947 to 1961, real output rose by 59 percent, but man-hours worked increased by only 3 percent, and the number of workers increased very little. This is due to the rising impact of the increase in productivity per hour, a result of the electronic revolution in the past fifteen years. This will continue, if not accelerate.

Economic growth will not solve the problem, although it will help. How do we cope with it? Miller suggests that a great many of the unemployed lack the training to work in this electronic age and quotes a labor market program that has been proposed in which education and reeducation play a substantial part. This would, indeed, help.

Concerning the solution of the Negro problem, Miller is not sanguine. He assumes that by 1980 42 percent of all Negro families will still be living in the South, where they will continue to be forced to deal with social discrimination—"a social disease that has been festering for 250 years." Even in the big cities to which Negroes migrate there is still discrimination in employment, housing, and education. Nevertheless, it is expected that discrimination will continue to be reduced slowly and that many Negroes will have improved their position by 1980.

Millionaires

Miller suggests that 30 percent of the population will have incomes over $10,000 by 1980. What will happen to millionaires and their wealth? They are on the increase. They may have tripled in the last ten years, although the population went up only 20 percent. There are 90,000 millionaires now. The average millionaire is sixty years old, but those with 10 million or more are only fifty-eight; the women are forty. Roughly 40 percent of *all* millionaires *are* women, and they owned, in 1958, 80 percent of estates over $10 million.[12] No one knows precisely why women are predominant in the millionaire class. Do they inherit this wealth or do young women marry old millionaires?

These millionaires are a post-World War II phenomenon. The new fortunes have been acquired largely through self-employment in a business. The tax laws are such that it would be difficult to acquire that much wealth from wages and salaries. The growth of this new group of millionaires has occurred because the government allows the owners of capital stock in a

[12] See Miller, "Millionaires Are a Dime a Dozen."

business to pay only 25 percent of the value of that stock in taxes, and to keep the remaining three-quarters of the profits when they sell the assets. There are tax advantages as well in real estate and insurance; there are depletion allowances in oil, mining, and timber that permit building up such assets.

Many of these men work long and hard to achieve millionaire status and are doing it in realms that are the product of the growth of population and technological change in industry. The increasing population wants more houses, more cars, more services and conveniences. Government tax monies frequently are distributed to sections of the population that could not otherwise buy these goods and services. They are part of the phenomenon of economic growth, and the government is now loath to change the tax system in any way that would impair this growth.

The number of millionaires is increasing, and Miller suggests that the new millions they own are usually earned, not inherited, because they create goods and services that the entire population can enjoy. They are the result of an expanding population and technological change in industry, of a dynamic economy in general. Should we, then, revise the capital gains tax—increase it, perhaps? Miller thinks not—it is "the price of prosperity in mid-century America."

The American distribution of income is still an unequal one, although with a decreasing poverty group and an increasing group at the higher income levels.

In addition, there is a growing class of millionaires. The income distribution continues to shift upward and to the right. Government aid is, in effect, given at both ends of the income distribution: to reduce poverty by methods such as subsidy, education, and retraining; and to increase the wealth of millionaires by the capital gains tax. Whether it would be in the interest of the government to increase this tax is a moot question. If a tax rise should reduce the millionaires sufficiently, this might cut into the stream of government subsidies that are used to boost up, take care of, and retrain the poor at the other end of the income distribution. It also might react disadvantageously upon the country's rate of growth.

It is to be expected that the income distribution will continue to remain unequal, though efforts will be made to lift up, by increasing government assistance, the poverty groups to a higher level. With respect to the millionaires, their wealth will not be interfered with, as long as the economy continues to grow. Should marked inflation occur, however, or the growth rate decline, then the story might well be different.

CHAPTER 6

Consumption and Economic Growth

The United States

One of the manifestations of economic growth is the changes in taste that occur in the consumer expenditure field. These are affected by the technological changes in the economy over time, which lead to the development of new products, products that are frequently made by different processes and with new materials. Such changes have occurred rather rapidly since World War II in the United States and have shown up for the most part in the increase in the service sectors of the economy, and in the substitution, in the production process, of materials such as plastics and synthetics for natural materials, or of nonferrous metals (especially aluminum) for steel.[1]

[1] Anne P. Carter, "The Economics of Technological Change," *Scientific American*, Vol. 214, No. 4 (April, 1966), 25–31.

There are many new and qualitatively different consumer products on the market. The question that con-
cerns us here is how these new products are introduced
to the consuming public. At what point do they enter
the market, by what process are they diffused, and
when is diffusion complete? Or, do they die out after
a trial period and never become diffused?

Dorothy Brady undertook to investigate the way in
which such new products reach certain consumers and
even finally spread throughout the consumer population as a whole.[2] She visualizes the process as consisting
of a series of stages.

The first stage is experimental. A new product is
developed by an industry for a particular economic
bracket of the consuming population, and these consumers give it a trial. The economic bracket may be
a high- or low-income bracket, although, in practice,
it has usually been one with high incomes. In the second stage, there is an extension of sales to other income
groups, by developing the product, by discovering
manufacturing efficiencies, by making new designs, etc.
In a later article,[3] Mrs. Brady includes a greater range
of prices as a key influence in the diffusion process.

[2] "The Diffusion of New Products and Their Impact on Consumer Expenditures." This investigation was made for the
Bureau of Labor Statistics Interagency Growth Study and never
published.

[3] With F. G. Adams, "The Diffusion of New Durable Goods
and Their Impact on Consumer Expenditures," *American Statistical Association, Proceedings of the Business and Economics
Statistics Section* (Washington, D.C., 1963), p. 76.

The third stage marks the diffusion of the sales of this commodity to more consumers in more diverse income brackets. And, at the fourth stage, a "saturation" point is reached at one or more economic levels (ideally, each level would have the same saturation point). Then, second-hand models may take the place of low-priced models; there may be a change in product design, which might take the place of the original one—and the diffusion process begins again.

If diffusion is completed, the volume of per capita expenditures for the new product would be equal among the economic groups—which implies, also, an equality in the price-income ratios in these groups. However, if an innovation is started in a high-income group and does not spread completely into other income groups, the quantities bought and the expenditures on the new product will vary greatly among the income groups. This diffusion process, over time, may be the result of changes in purchasing power or of real income in the income groups or of changes in taste that are quite independent of changes in income.

This model has been set up in statistical form and applied to a number of innovations for food products, automobiles, household durable goods, and clothing. There is a very enlightening study of the piano, for example, which is one of those durables that never became completely diffused throughout the population. The American Statistical Association article deals only with consumer durables, such as television sets, mechanical refrigerators, and washing machines, and emphasizes the role of price in the diffusion process. It is of interest to note that television sets are the only consumer durable to show a completely full cycle of diffusion in the population of the United States since World War II.

Technological change and changes in taste have also been widespread with respect to the consumption of food in this country over the past eighty-odd years. Food is, of course, a necessity of life as we literally have to eat to live. Food is also one of the major consumer expenditure items for any family or individual; and, for years, it ranked first in the percentage of income (or total consumer expenditures) spent in the average family budget. As we saw in Chapter 3, it was displaced by the household complex and went down to second place in the 1960–1961 consumer expenditure survey.

The changes in the consumption of food since the late nineteenth century involve a number of elements. There have been changes in the total amount spent and in the amount spent relative to income. The structure of the "food bundle" has altered: The amount of money spent on particular foods has changed; new and different food products have been introduced. The physical amount of food purchased—as measured by caloric content—is not the same. Changes in the techniques of producing and processing foods have brought on structural changes in the food complex and introduced changes in taste. Many other factors, such as social and health influences, have also been at work.

A detailed study of American dietary changes from 1879 to 1959 was undertaken by Merrill Bennett and Rosamund Peirce, of the Stanford Food Research Institute.[4] They found that total food calories per capita per day decreased from 3,741 to 3,187 over the whole period. There was a decline of 550 calories, or 15 percent, from 1879 to 1958, and a 10 percent decrease (350 calories) from 1910 to 1918. Their analysis of the possible causes for this decline listed the reduction in physical activity of people during the period, the decrease in exposure to cold, and, in recent years, dieting on the basis of medical advice.

In breaking down the food group, they discovered a distinct shift from starchy to nonstarchy foods. Non-starchy foods increased from 1,750 to 2,400 calories per capita per day, whereas starchy foods decreased from 1,976 to 761 calories, with the greatest decline shown in the consumption of corn meal and wheat flour. All the constituents of the nonstarch group—meats, fats, milk, sugar, and vegetables and fruits—shared in the increase. The authors explain this shift as a change in taste, implemented by a "persistent" increase in per capita income. They note, too, that the change occurred despite the fact that the prices of nonstarchy foods went up, on the whole, over the period. They do not believe that advertising or nutritional advice could possibly explain this shift.

[4] Merrill Bennett and Rosamund Peirce, "Change in the American National Diet, 1879–1959," *Stanford Food Research Institute Studies* (May, 1961).

This change in the structure of food consumption does, indeed, appear to represent a real change in taste. The main reasons may be found in the rapid economic growth of the United States and the consistent increase in real income and the level of living over the long range. There was, too, a greater mobility among the population, both socially and in means of transportation. Technological change helped, especially in improvements in product quality among the nonstarch products: better cattle, fruits, vegetables, poultry, and the like. There was also an improvement in processing to maintain product quality over time, in canning, freezing, and packaging. Now the consumption of seasonal foods has been spread out through the year by fast transportation from the growing areas. Lobsters from Maine appear in Denver, Colorado; fruits and vegetables from California and Florida are flown or trucked to the East.

Since World War II medical advice has had some effect on the dietary proclivities of many in the population. If the income distribution continues to shift upward and to the right and if poverty is eliminated, what, then, will happen to the structure of the consumption of food? Will medical considerations have greater impact? Will still other technological and social factors change the dietary pattern again?

Other Countries

In commemorating the centenary of Ernst Engel's birth, Hendrik Houthakker undertook to investigate for a number of countries whether Engel's laws, as they are commonly called (although Engel was actually responsible for only the one on food) still function. He was interested in finding out whether expenditure patterns are comparable for countries at widely different stages of economic growth, and also whether it might be possible to infer such laws, for countries that have no data on consumer expenditures, from the relationship in other countries in comparable stages of growth.

Houthakker dealt with the four major classes of expenditure in the consumer budget: food (excluding alcohol), housing (including fuel and light), clothing (including footwear), and miscellaneous (or all other items) for some thirty-seven countries in various stages of economic development. These data were largely post-World War II data, of the cross-section variety, in which expenditures are grouped by income class for a particular year. Houthakker used total expenditures instead of total income as the basis of his analysis, in the same fashion as was done in the discussion of consumer expenditure surveys in Chapter 3. In some ways, total expenditures form a more reliable base than total income, as they tend to be relatively more stable from year to year. The measure of elasticity was then derived by using a double logarithmic equation that included family size as well as total group expenditures.[5] In

[5] See Hendrik Houthakker, "An International Comparison of Household Expenditure Patterns, Commemorating the Centenary of Engel's Law," *Econometrica* (October, 1957).

other words, *partial* elasticities for both the expenditure groups and the family size were derived.

The countries in this study were widely diversified, ranging from the United States, Canada, the Netherlands, West Germany, Japan, Italy, Brazil, Ghana, Portugal, India to Guatemala, the Philippines, the United Kingdom, and many others.

The results were as follows, using the above partial elasticities for the budgetary items as measures of the four classes of consumer expenditures:

(1) *Food.* The elasticities in this group were all significantly less than 1, but with a very substantial range of values; that is, outlays on food tended to be a declining portion of the total as the total increased. The highest was Poland, with 0.731; the lowest, 0.344, was for a British middle-class survey. The elasticities for the United States and Canada were relatively high in comparison with other countries, namely, 0.7 and 0.6, respectively.

(2) *Clothing.* All elasticities were greater than unity; outlays on clothing increased as a percentage of the total, and no particular pattern was noted.

(3) *Housing.* The elasticities were below 1 for the most part, with considerable variation.

(4) *Miscellaneous.* All elasticities were greater than unity; those for Canada and the United States were the only ones below 1.4, being 1.1 and 1.2, respectively.

In deriving partial elasticities for *both* family size and consumption for the four main consumer categories, the two variables were included in the same regression equation, so that any interaction between them would appear in the statistical results. The partial elasticities for family size were extremely irregular for clothing and housing, although regularity was apparent for food and the miscellaneous category. In combining the partial elasticities for the main consumer expenditure groups with those for family size, therefore, clothing and miscellaneous were counted as zero for the latter. In the absence of consumer expenditure data for a particular country, Houthakker thinks that one "would not go far astray" in using the partial elasticities (shown in Table 8) for the principal expenditure categories and family size.

TABLE 8

| | *Partial Elasticities of* | |
	TOTAL EXPENDITURE	FAMILY SIZE
Food	0.6	0.3
Clothing	1.2	0
Housing	0.8	0
All other	1.6	—0.4

SOURCE: Based on statistics from Hendrik Houthakker, "An International Comparison of Household Expenditure Patterns, Commemorating the Centenary of Engel's Law," *Econometrica* (October, 1957), p. 550.

Although Houthakker would prefer to have consumer expenditure surveys available, he suggests that, in their absence, the above elasticities might be used to provide a rough indication of the stage of economic growth a country has achieved.

However, there may be some question as to how useful these aggregate measures are for actual policy formation. While they may provide a rough indication of the stage of economic growth in a country, one is frequently interested in more specific items in dealing with problems of economic development. It is often necessary to know what kinds of food, houses, clothes, and miscellaneous expenditures are purchased in order to measure the repercussions of consumer expenditures upon the productive system, and vice versa.

The U.S.S.R.

In recent years the Russians have turned their attention to problems in the area of consumption. There are many Soviet economic articles on both the theoretical and empirical aspects of the growth of consumer demand. Until now, Soviet efforts have been largely concentrated on the supply side of the economy and the development of a highly industrialized system, with emphasis on heavy industry. Much has been accomplished in this area, and Russia is now second only to the United States in industrialization, nuclear power, and the like. They can well afford, therefore, to attend to the consumption demands of the population. In fact, they must do so, with the rise in the income and education of their consuming public and the increasing contacts with Western ideas.[6]

[6] This is not unlike the change in emphasis in our own economic thinking—with a lag of about thirty years, as shown in the early pages of this book.

It seems clear that the Russian planning system in the production and marketing of consumer goods needs to be revised. Both the production and the consumption of consumer goods are controlled by the government—retailing, wholesaling, and manufacturing levels and geographical location. Consumer goods are distributed by going from the factory to the wholesaler to the retailer and finally to the consumer. The main trade networks are government stores (urban), cooperative stores, and the kolkhoz, or collective farm markets. Although the Russians are attempting to improve their distribution system by decentralization and better-quality goods, it is not easy. Central planning becomes more and more difficult as production increases and a greater variety of consumer goods becomes available. Consumers are also becoming more demanding and frequently refuse to buy goods that have been contracted for by the stores.[7]

At the same time, economists have become greatly interested in the analysis of consumer demand. The July, 1964, issue of *Problems of Economics* was devoted entirely to this subject, and in May, 1965, another article dealt with the material conditions of family life in Ashkhabad. Interestingly enough, the key variable in this article was the extent of the education of the wife and mother, which did appear to influence the acquisition of so-called cultural goods.

Economists are studying the relation of changes in

[7] See Marshall I. Goldman, *Soviet Marketing—Distribution in a Controlled Economy* (New York: Free Press, 1963).

consumption to changes in income, family size, age, education, and social and cultural influences, which are very different in the various republics of the Soviet Union. Consumer expenditure surveys have been re-discovered, and many budget studies are being made and analyzed in research centers and universities throughout the Soviet Union.

All of this recent work on consumption is, of course, phrased in terms of Marxism. It is represented as the carrying-out of true Marxist ideas. In fact, however, the results being attained by this research are very simi-lar to those that occur in the United States and other capitalist countries. The proportion of income spent on food decreases as income rises; there is an increase in the shares of clothing, linen, footwear, furniture, and "articles for cultural purposes." There is great empha-sis in these available studies on social and cultural levels.

Some of these studies indicate that many of the Rus-sian families are at a rather low level as far as the ac-quisition of furniture and durable goods is concerned. Presumably, this will change as a greater amount of attention is paid to the production of consumer goods in the Russian economy. As a matter of fact, the situa-tion *is* changing now, as the Russians attempt to stimu-late the consumer goods industries to produce more and better durable goods, clothing, and the like.

In a recent five-volume study of *New Directions in the Soviet Economy* prepared for the Joint Economic

Committee of the United States Congress, the question of what is happening to consumption in the Soviet economy is closely examined.[8] Per capita consumption has been growing at an average annual rate of 5 percent from 1950 to 1958, and somewhat less than that afterward, with the result that Soviet consumption increased from 27 percent of United States consumption in 1955 to 31 percent in 1964. Relative consumption of food has declined over time; that of services has been higher, as has the consumption of soft goods. The consumption of durable goods has increased the most, although at a declining rate of increase since 1950.

A tremendous pent-up demand for consumer durables exists, which means that their producers must compete with industries that make machines for industrial development. Long waiting lists exist for the purchases of cars, refrigerators, washing machines, and many other durables.

This spurt in consumption is in large part due to the great increase in money income that has taken place. Disposable income has grown by nearly 200 percent since 1950. But since the late fifties consumers have not been willing to buy shoddy or poorly designed textiles, clothing, or footwear; so the inventories of

[8] 89th Congress, 2nd Session, 1966. Three articles on consumption are included in Section 4: David W. Bronson and Barbara S. Severin, "Recent Trends in Consumption and Disposable Money Income in the U.S.S.R."; T. Sosnovy, "Housing Conditions and Urban Development in the U.S.S.R."; I. Erro, "Economic Reform in the Soviet Consumer Industries."

these goods have become very large. Price reductions and installment credit have not ameliorated the situation. A solution to this problem was therefore tackled at the plant level.

Two clothing plants were selected, in 1964, to experiment with production plans based on direct contracts with retail stores and using established profits as the chief measure of plant performance and managerial rewards. Six months later, this experiment was expanded to include over 400 plants in light industry and the food industry. The initial experiment with the Bol'shevichka plant in Moscow and with the Mayak plant in Gorky was a considerable success. These two plants, the first of which produced men's suits, the second, women's and children's clothing, made many changes in plant operation and management such as new design departments, quality control, smaller production runs, and direct delivery to retail outlets. The usual wholesale network was bypassed entirely.

The expansion of the new plan in January, 1965, to 400 plants has not been entirely successful. For one thing, the host of officials in the retail and wholesale network, as well as many local authorities, got in the way of smooth operation. However, in October, 1965, Premier Aleksei Kosygin, in a speech before the Supreme Soviet, recommended the use of profit and bonuses, direct contracting, and the value of sales rather than gross output as an indicator of an industry's performance, and proposed that interest be charged on capital. Stronger centralization was urged, and the regional officials who directed industries under the Khrushchev plan of 1957 were thrown out in favor of new national ministries.

This brief—and inadequate—account of changes in the Soviet industrial mechanism appears to show that industries in Russia are undergoing substantial change. And this change began with the consumer goods industries because of refusals to buy the goods produced and sold in many of the government stores. Now consumers are being urged to buy houses, durable goods, and many other commodities.[9] One-third of the housing space in Russia is "in the personal possession of the citizens." A number of questions have been raised in the journals and newspapers. Is such personal possession consistent with communism? The official explanation says that it is; to own a house or a car does *not*

[9] A brief trip to Leningrad (three days) in the summer of 1967 indicated that many consumer goods, except for clothes and possibly apartments, are still in short supply. The streets of Leningrad were practically bare of cars except for a few in official use. Rather large, ugly, concrete housing structures provided space for apartments. The clothing situation seemed much better. The young in Leningrad appeared stylishly dressed (although I did not have any chance to examine the materials used); while walking around the city one evening, I observed some girls in mini-skirts! At Petrovorets' Park, the former summer palace of the Czar and now a recreational area for the people of Leningrad, the clothes of the families and young were also in style. In northern Poland, too, the people seemed well-dressed. The guide mentioned to us that the state was now providing more stylish clothing than previously.

mean that one has "private property," but "personal property" and such "personal affluence" is by no means inconsistent with communism.[10]

Communist China

The situation in Communist China[11] is not completely comparable to that in Russia, despite the fact that the Chinese copied a good deal from the Soviets, particularly in the 1950's. During the 1960's China appears to have been pursuing a policy of more balanced growth, especially in connection with the consumer goods industries. Large investments were made in textiles and clothing, partly in order to gain badly needed foreign exchange. There are some well-equipped factories in these areas. The Chinese also appear to be interested in supplying more and better consumer goods to the general population. Their stores have a quite wide variety of consumer goods, even in places where foreigners do not usually go. Dr. Richman comments that "The largest Soviet department store—GUM in Moscow—does not come close to the large department stores in Peking, Shanghai, or Tientsin in

[10] Peter Grose, "Personal, Comrades, Is Not Private," *The New York Times Magazine,* August 27, 1966.

[11] The information on China, which may now be outdated, is taken from Barry M. Richman, "Capitalists and Managers in Communist China," *Harvard Business Review* (January-February, 1967).

terms of variety or quality of consumer goods available." [12]

Chinese society seems to be quite different from the Russian in many ways. The Chinese have not thrown out the capitalists—they are used—but the factories are usually dominated by party followers. The money incentive is not used to separate workers and managers. There is no "elite" in China where upper-level managers get better housing and are given a car, as there is in the Soviet Union. It should be noted that this managerial group in Russia is provided with many consumer benefits by the state, which must, in effect, be added to the consumer goods that they buy from their own incomes.

In Communist China, although consumer demands have been considered at an earlier stage of industrial development than in Russia, a choice must be made between Maoist doctrine and mature industrial development. If China is to become a completely modern economy, technical know-how must be emphasized and pecuniary incentives used. This is not in line with Maoist doctrine. Russia has already overthrown the tenets of Marxism which conflict with mature industrial development. Will China do the same?

As an economy grows and incomes increase, so will consumption, irrespective of the political philosophy that rules. This process can be deferred, it is true, as

[12] *Ibid.,* p. 72.

it was in Russia while its industrial system was being built up; but a point is eventually reached where more than minimum consumer demands must be met. Economic growth in itself tends to force the adoption of certain economic mechanisms, irrespective of avowed political systems. One has only to compare, for instance, Japan (under an emperor), communist Russia, Communist China, and the democratic United States. All of these countries are facing an expansion in consumer demands brought forth by the development of a highly technical industrial system. Whether Communist China will continue to develop is, at the moment, a moot question.

Consumer demands, however, are not as easy to control as producer demands. Changes in taste introduce an unstable, noneconomic element. Why is it that many new commodities have not caught on or have not been thoroughly diffused in the United States? Why are the Russians having so much trouble with their marketing system that they are being forced to adapt it to consumer desires? There are some consumer goods that many consumers simply will not buy.

Houthakker has shown that there is a certain stability in countries at various stages of economic growth with respect to the four main categories of consumer expenditures: food, housing, clothes, and miscellaneous items. Within those categories, there need not be—and frequently there is not—any kind of stability for individual items of consumer expenditure.

Bibliography

For the analysis of the consumption function and its role in the economic system, John Maynard Keynes' *The General Theory of Employment, Interest, and Money* (New York: Harcourt, Brace & World, 1936) is still the basic work. The relative income hypothesis is taken up in *Income, Saving and the Theory of Consumer Behavior* (Cambridge, Mass.: Harvard University Press, 1949), by James S. Duesenberry. Milton Friedman's *A Theory of the Consumption Function* (Princeton, N.J.: Princeton University Press, 1957) presents the case for the use of permanent income in the consumption function and is still controversial.

John R. Hicks has set forth the modern view of consumer preference theory for the individual in *Value and Capital* (New York: Oxford, 1939). In *Family Composition and Consumption* (Amsterdam: North Holland Publishing Company, 1962), Martin H. David attempts to expand consumer preference theory to deal with the family as a unit rather than the individual.

James N. Morgan, Martin H. David, Wilbur J. Cohen, and Harvey E. Brazer, in *Income and Welfare in the United States* (New York: McGraw-Hill, 1962), give a detailed statistical analysis of the factors affecting our income and welfare. Also useful in this field are the annual *Economic Reports of the President* and the summary reports of the Bureau of Labor Statistics, some of which are referred to in Chapter 3.

Of Time, Work and Leisure (New York: Twentieth Century Fund, 1962), by Sebastian de Grazia, is a fascinating book that discusses many of the problems of "hours away from work" taken up in Chapter 4.

Herman Miller's *Rich Man Poor Man* (New York: Crowell-Collier, 1964) is an excellent and readable analysis of the factors affecting the size distribution of income in the United States.

For a survey of changes now taking place in the industrial organization of the U.S.S.R., *New Directions in the Soviet Economy,* Parts I–IV, prepared for the use of the Joint Economic Committee, 89th Congress of the United States, 2nd Session 1966, provides an excellent analysis of Russian attempts to catch up with the West on consumer goods, especially consumer durables. It should be noted that *The New York Times* has been currently reporting on the changes in the production system, especially durables, now occurring in the U.S.S.R. in 1967.

Glossary of Economists

A number of well-known economists have been referred to in the text. Some of them and the institutions with which they are connected are listed below:

Professor Dorothy S. Brady — *University of Pennsylvania, Philadelphia, Pennsylvania.*

Professor Martin H. David — *University of Wisconsin, Madison, Wisconsin.*

Professor James S. Duesenberry — *Harvard University, Cambridge, Massachusetts. On leave 1966–1968, at the Council of Economic Advisers, Washington, D.C.*

Professor Milton Friedman — *University of Chicago, Chicago, Illinois.*

Professor John R. Hicks — *All Souls College, Oxford, England.*

Professor Hendrik S. Houthakker — *Harvard University, Cambridge, Massachusetts. On leave at the Council of Economic Advisers, 1967–1968, Washington, D.C.*

Professor Irving B. Kravis — *University of Pennsylvania, Philadelphia, Pennsylvania.*

Professor Simon Kuznets — *Harvard University, Cambridge, Massachusetts.*

Professor Vernon Lippitt — *University of Rochester, Rochester, New York.*

Herman P. Miller — *Special Assistant to the Director of the Bureau of the Census, Washington, D.C.*

Professor James N. Morgan   *University of Michigan, Ann Arbor, Michigan.*

Dr. Barry M. Richman   *Chairman of the International Business Program and of the Management Theory and Industrial Relations Division, Graduate School of Business Administration, University of California, Los Angeles, California.*

Professor Paul Samuelson   *Massachusetts Institute of Technology, Cambridge, Massachusetts.*

Index

About the Author

Elizabeth W. Gilboy has had a long and distinguished career in economic scholarship. A graduate of Barnard with honors in economics and membership in Phi Beta Kappa and with a Ph.D. degree from Radcliffe, she has been on the faculties of Harvard, Radcliffe, and Wellesley. She is the author of two books and a contributor to seven others. Her articles in scholarly journals comprise a long list, most of them concerned with various aspects of the subject of this book.

During World War II, Mrs. Gilboy served with distinction with the Office of Strategic Services in Washington, and she has also traveled widely as an economic consultant on government and educational matters, including a visit to Yugoslavia at the invitation of the Yugoslav Statistical Association.

She has worked closely with Wassily Leontief on input-output economics and is currently Associate Director of the Harvard Economic Research Project and Lecturer in Economics at Harvard University in Cambridge, Massachusetts.

A Note on the Type

The text of this book was set on the Linotype in Baskerville. Linotype Baskerville is a facsimile cutting from type cast from the original matrices of a face designed by John Baskerville. The original face was the forerunner of the "modern" group of type faces.

John Baskerville (1706–75), of Birmingham, England, a writing-master, with a special renown for cutting inscriptions in stone, began experimenting about 1750 with punch-cutting and making typographical material. It was not until 1757 that he published his first work. His types, at first criticized, in time were recognized as both distinct and elegant, and his types as well as his printing were greatly admired.

Composed, printed, and bound by The Colonial Press, Inc., Clinton, Mass. Design by Leon Bolognese